A great book! ... kman offers an edifying collection ... any Catholic women. Their stories are inspiring and bear witness to the reality that when the feminine heart is at prayer, the world is a more lovely and beautiful place.

Never underestimate the power of women at prayer! Were it not for the many prayerful women in my life — the Virgin Mary, my earthly mother, five Filipino prayer warriors, and my best friend — I wouldn't be the man I am today. This book blessed my life, and it will be a tremendous blessing for all who read it.

—**Fr. Donald Calloway, M.I.C.**
Author, *Champions of the Rosary*

Kathleen Beckman has put together a beautiful collection of personal stories and teachings on prayer. *When Women Pray* is a forum for a compelling group of lay Catholic women leaders. To read this is to sit down with an articulate gathering of sincere disciples pouring out the fruit of their conversations with the Lord. Together, they disclose a wisdom that is at once learned and practical, insightful and accessible, at times lighthearted but always reverent. One finds here, expressed in words, the profound solidarity that women of prayer share together, a tender strength that the Church needs today more than ever. Highly recommended!

—**Dr. Anthony Lilles**
Author, *Fire from Above: Christian Contemplation and Mystical Wisdom*;
Avila Institute of Spiritual Formation

Women were created, as St. John Paul II identifies, with a space inside for another. Through the chapters contained in this book, these women leaders give birth and share with others various aspects of prayer that they have carried within. It is not only important that women's voices be heard in today's world of pragmatic interests; it is vital for our human striving toward fulfillment in the Divine. A thoughtful, inspiring book!

—**Sister Joseph Andrew Bogdanowicz, O.P.**
Vocation Director, Dominican Sisters of Mary, Mother of the Eucharist

In this book, eleven women of prayer articulate how they pray, what prayer means to them, and the fruits associated with an active prayer life. *When Women Pray* is inspiring, full of substance, and frankly, difficult to put down. The reader will be enriched by the contributions of the individual writers and will indeed learn practical ways to authentically live his or her spiritual life. I highly recommend this work.

—**Msgr. Stephen S. Doktorczyk, J.C.D.**
Official at the Holy See; Author, *Persistent Disobedience to Church Authority: History, Analysis and Application of Canon 1371, 2º*

When Women Pray is a beautiful and timely book. Readers will find reflections that shed light on the myriad ways that God communes with feminine hearts. The feminine vocation is mirrored in the Trinity's invitation to the Virgin Mary: The Father asked, "Daughter, will you become the Mother of my only-begotten Son?" The Son asked, "Will you become my Mother and the mother of mankind?" The Holy Spirit asked, "Beloved, will you become my Spouse?" Daughter, mother, and spouse are a woman's calling to profound spiritual life in Him. This book affirms that God desires to penetrate our hearts deeply and inspires us to pray always, so, with Mary, we will bear greater fruit for eternal life.

—**Mother Dolores Marie, P.C.P.A.**
Our Lady of the Angels Monastery, Hanceville, Alabama; Contributing Author, *Manual for Eucharistic Adoration*

I always say that when faith-filled prayerful women get together—watch out! With God's amazing grace, these women have the power to change the world! Author Kathleen Beckman skillfully compiles the intimate stories of eleven faithful women guaranteed to inspire you to keep your lamp lit, penetrating the darkness of the world and aiding others to find their way to heaven. I love this book!

—**Donna-Marie Cooper O'Boyle**
EWTN TV host, speaker, and award-winning author of more than twenty books, including *The Kiss of Jesus* and *Feeding Your Family's Soul*

When Women Pray

Other books by Kathleen Beckman
from Sophia Institute Press:

Praying for Priests
A Mission for the New Evangelization

God's Healing Mercy
Finding Your Path to Forgiveness, Peace, and Joy

When
Women
PRAY

Eleven Catholic Women
on the Power of Prayer

EDITED BY KATHLEEN BECKMAN, L.H.S.

SOPHIA INSTITUTE PRESS
Manchester, New Hampshire

Nihil obstat: Fr. Hugh Barbour, O. Praem., *Censor Librorum*

Imprimatur: Most Reverend Kevin W. Vann, J.C.D., D.D.,
Bishop of Orange, February 24, 2017

Sophia Institute Press
Box 5284, Manchester, NH 03108
1-800-888-9344
www.SophiaInstitute.com

Sophia Institute Press® is a registered trademark of Sophia Institute.

Library of Congress Cataloging-in-Publication Data

Names: Beckman, Kathleen, editor.
Title: When women pray : eleven Catholic women on the power of prayer /
 edited by Kathleen Beckman.
Description: Manchester, New Hampshire : Sophia Institute Press, 2017.
Identifiers: LCCN 2017002459 | ISBN 9781622823864 (pbk. : alk. paper)
Subjects: LCSH: Catholic women — Religious life. | Prayer — Catholic Church.
Classification: LCC BX2353 .W44 2017 | DDC 248.3/2082 — dc23 LC record avail-able at https://lccn.loc.gov/2017002459

First printing

To my parents, Richard and Gloria,
first teachers of the Faith

Contents

Appendices

Foreword

Somewhere in the secret chambers of a woman's heart there is a gentle, persistent longing for holiness. We use various words to describe this longing: a desire for depth, for wholeness; a hunger for something more meaningful than our daily routine, something greater than ourselves. Sometimes we become aware of this longing during those precious moments of peace and leisure. At other times the yearning makes itself known during barren days of angst or during crushing periods of darkness.

Why such a persistent longing in a woman's heart? How does she satisfy the longing during all the fluctuating seasons of the soul?

The answers to these two questions are intrinsically linked. If you understand the answer to the first question, you have already solved the problem of the second question.

The persistent longing was actually embedded in our DNA the moment we were conceived. We were made *in* Love, *by* Love, and *for* Love. God, who is total, infinite, unchanging Love, thought of you, and His Heart was flooded with love for you. He created you that He might carry you in His love, that you might be in intimate relationship with Him, talk with Him, allow Him to love you, to touch you, to speak with you. You didn't do anything to deserve this love. You can't *do* anything to lose His love. It is yours. Forever. No matter what. That is why we are never completely fulfilled except when we are close to God. That is why we experience the longing, that He might fill it as only He can.

How do we weather the seasons of the soul? As best we can. We are frail human beings. That is all we ever will be. Our frailty poses no obstacle whatsoever to God.

The Lord cannot take His eyes off us; it is impossible for Him to tear His Heart away from us. We are never alone. But so often we can feel alone and can become absorbed in our little world. That is because we can forget the unimaginable power and blessing that belongs to us: we are able to communicate with God.

In the Old Testament we discover women who prayed, women whose influence continues throughout the centuries even to today: Esther and the power of one woman's intercession; Judith's audacious faith and unstoppable resolve; Deborah's far-reaching influence as the only woman judge. In the New Testament we come upon that unknown child whose simple trust in the Word of the Lord brought about her unconditional Fiat, and the world was changed forever. These women spoke with God, they listened to Him and responded in faith.

Our Lord does not need special people or extraordinary circumstances. Look at the people He chose: a Hebrew girl, a carpenter, a few fishermen, Magdalene, a group of women who accompanied Him. Holiness is integrated within the routine and commonplace, within the scheduled and unscheduled happenings during each day's unfolding. In that unfolding, our individual paths are often fraught with suffering and pain, that is true, but they are also emblazoned with the fire of love that overcomes and prevails.

This fire is what Lady Kathleen Beckman captures in her latest book, *When Women Pray*. We encounter joy and peace in the surrendered heart. A broken heart becomes the seedbed of new life. There is an unspoken confidence flowing from the sure and certain knowledge that God accompanies us every step of the way.

In the early 1950s Venerable Archbishop Fulton J. Sheen made a compelling statement on his popular television program *Life Is Worth Living.*

"The level of any civilization
is always the level of its womanhood."

The testimonies in this book are unique and personal. The authors share real struggles, tragic pain, palpable triumphs. These women have one thing in common: in the midst of their very human condition they learned to pray. It is that simple. Each woman emerges as a source of life to others. Each touches other hearts and raises the level of our civilization.

This book is an invitation to step into your rightful place alongside women who have prayed through the centuries; women who have heard the beating Heart of God and changed the world forever.

Sister Regina Marie Gorman, O.C.D.
Vicar General, Carmelite Sisters
of the Most Sacred Heart of Los Angeles

Acknowledgments

A debt of gratitude is owed to the magnanimous president of Sophia Institute Press, Charlie McKinney. Your positive response to my initial inspiration encouraged me to move forward with this collaborative book. Thank you also to the talented Sophia Institute Press team, Nora, Molly, Aja, and Michael. It's my privilege and joy to work with you.

I am truly humbled and grateful for the creative feminine genius of the ten contributing authors. I have long admired your respective work and am edified to see God's hand on you and your apostolates. Thanks to your generous yes, and the Holy Spirit's anointing, a beautiful bouquet is formed here. Together we present it to the Lord and His Church, to our sisters in Christ.

With gratitude, I acknowledge a trinity of priests, Msgr. Stephen Doktorczyk, Fr. Raymond Skonezny, and Fr. Charles Cortinovis for much-needed prayer support, theological advice, and editing. Also, I thank Bishop Kevin W. Vann and Fr. Hugh Barbour, O. Praem. for your review and support. These priests make all the difference in the world, and in my life of faith.

God reward my beloved family and friends who blessed me throughout this project.

Most Holy Trinity, thank You for the grace to carry this work to fruition. Please use this humble offering to stir up an army of faith-filled women to keep a vigil of prayer — with Mary.

When Women Pray

Prayer, Perseverance, and Preparedness

The inspiration for this collaborative book came during a Eucharistic holy hour while I was contemplating the parable of the ten virgins.

> Ten maidens … took their lamps and went to meet the bridegroom. Five of them were foolish, and five were wise. For when the foolish took their lamps, they took no oil with them; but the wise took flasks of oil with their lamps. As the bridegroom was delayed, they all slumbered and slept. But at midnight there was a cry, "Behold, the bridegroom! Come out to meet him." Then all those maidens rose and trimmed their lamps. And the foolish said to the wise, "Give us some of your oil, for our lamps are going out." But the wise replied, "Perhaps there will not be enough for us and for you; go rather to the dealers and buy for yourselves." And while they went to buy, the bridegroom came, and those who were ready went in with him to the marriage feast; and the door was shut. Afterward the other maidens came also, saying, "Lord, lord, open to us." But he replied, "Truly, I say to you, I do

not know you." Watch therefore, for you know neither the day nor the hour. (Matt 25:1–13)

In reflecting on this parable, I imagined the combined wisdom of women of prayer.

A few months later, a retreat master preached on this parable. He said that the five wise virgins could not share their oil with the five foolish virgins because the oil represented a "relationship with God." Thus, when the foolish virgins came knocking on the door, the Lord replied, "I do not know you." Absent the oil of prayer, there was no relationship with God in place.

Can you imagine the anguish of being locked out of the Lord's wedding banquet? (Women love weddings!) Worse is hearing Christ say, "I do not know you." This is a sobering reality.

The value we place on prayer amounts to a decision to choose wisdom or foolishness. It's that simple. The oil of prayer is necessary (it is a holy duty), is wise (it is the will of God), is worth the effort (it is fruitful), and empowers the active apostolate (the contemplatives in action). But for prayer we need courage and encouragement.

The challenge is to keep our lamps full of the oil of prayer while living and working in a culture of hedonistic noise. In twenty-five years of ministry to Catholic women (thanks to *Magnificat*), I've met thousands of women who embrace the challenge of prayer with heroic resiliency. When apathy or lethargy tempts, grace quickens us to resist and to persist in prayer.

Gathered here are poignant stories and simple, profound teachings on prayer from two generations of Catholic women. Foundresses of international apostolates, theologians and professors, media hosts, reporters, and prolific authors — they are *contemplatives in action*. Not experts on prayer, but faithful and persevering are these daughters, sisters, wives, single women, widows, mothers, and grandmothers who candidly share how they pray in the midst of their busy schedules and overcome the battle of prayer.

Our goal for this book is to strengthen an army of praying women united for the many spiritual and temporal needs of the human family.

Prayer lights the lamp of our life, cuts through the darkness, and illumines the narrow road. Women perceive the light and also intuit the darkness that encroaches on every area of our lives: self-image, marriage, children, relationships, work environments, the apostolate, the Church, and the world. Through prayer, we perceive human need and receive the grace to respond as God wills.

Venerable Archbishop Fulton Sheen said, "To a great extent the level of any civilization is the level of its womanhood."[1] Between 1962 and 1965, Bishop Sheen attended all the sessions of the Second Vatican Council. He worked closely with then Father Joseph Ratzinger, who was a theological expert on the commission for mission, and who later became Pope Benedict XVI.[2]

At the solemn closing ceremony of the Second Vatican Council, on December 8, 1965, the Council Fathers gave a prophetic message to women, which says, in part:

> But the hour is coming, in fact has come, when the vocation of woman is being achieved in its fullness, the hour in which woman acquires in the world an influence, an

---

[1] Fulton J. Sheen, *Life Is Worth Living*, "Living and Knowing."

[2] "Biographical Profile of Fulton J. Sheen," Catholic University of America website, http://fulton-sheen.cua.edu/bio/index.cfm.

effect, and a power never hitherto achieved. That is why, at this moment when the human race is undergoing so deep a transformation, women impregnated with the spirit of the Gospel can do much to aid mankind in not falling.

This message seems urgent. There is a need for women who are impregnated with the spirit of the Gospel, in other words, Marian women. Will humanity be transformed for light or for darkness? According to the Church, women have a profound influence in the outcome, in part because of our role in the domestic church. When we stand in defense of faith, marriage, and family, we magnify God's light and push back darkness. It takes prayer to be who we are called to be in an anti-Christian culture.

As evidenced in the stories in this book, in one vocation, there are likely several missions. In the life of Mary, the lives of women saints, and the lives of the writers of this book, God has called forth many missions for women infused with the oil of prayer.

In Scripture, we learn, "Whenever Moses held up his hand, Israel prevailed; and whenever he lowered his hand, Amalek prevailed" (Exod. 17:11). Prayer is work. When Moses got tired of holding up his arms, his friends held them up for him. They persisted in prayer, and victory was theirs. As the world grows cynical about prayer, let us hold fast to God's Word, which exhorts us to pray unceasingly (see Thess. 5:17).

Women have a gift for intercessory prayer, as evidenced within these pages. The vocation of woman as Christ-bearer, life-bearer, and cooperator with God's initiatives can be fully realized only through prayer—deeper mystical communion with the Father, the Son, and the Holy Spirit. We hope that the stirring witnesses of prayer and teaching in this book will help to deepen your encounter with God.

Let us keep our lamps filled so that we may join the ranks of the Church's wise women and be prepared for the Bridegroom and the best wedding banquet ever. Sisters, what are we going to wear to the Bridegroom's banquet? An elegant garment of prayer, patiently woven with threads of faith, hope, and love.

To facilitate personal or group retreats, each chapter ends with spiritual exercises titled "Ponder, Practice, Pray" coupled with "Feminine Wisdom" from women saints. In the appendices you'll find Romano Guardini's teachings on the difference between personal and liturgical prayer and on the essentialness of prayer to health.

Although there is a wealth of catechesis on prayer within, this book is not intended to be a prayer manual per se. The key word in the title is *when*: when women pray, what happens? You'll discover the surprising answer within the pages of this book.

Kathleen Beckman
Epiphany 2017

CHAPTER 1

The Marian Heart Prays

Kathleen Beckman

In the elegant film *Full of Grace*,[3] there's a scene in which Mary speaks to the Apostles, who have assembled to be with her shortly before her Assumption. Her words are delivered like a sage maternal prayer, "My children, if you do nothing more in this life, remember the moment Jesus first looked upon you. Your soul rejoiced, for salvation was upon you. Darkness was lifted, and you saw the great Light. Remember that moment, and everything you do will glorify God."

From my earliest memory, Mary has similarly mothered me to remember Jesus, and in remembering, there is communion. Mary coaches us to keep alive the defining moments of our walk with God. Do you recall that moment when Jesus first looked upon you with such a loving gaze that you knew He was real, and you felt that you were lovable and acceptable? Do you remember how your heart responded?

Since I'm the oldest of five children and the only girl, Mary was not only my mother, but also my sister and my friend. Mary

---

[3] *Full of Grace: The Story of Mary, the Mother of Jesus*, directed by Andrew Hyatt (Outside da Box, 2015), http://fullofgracefilm.com.

mentored me to cling not to her, but to Jesus. As I matured in faith, in my mid-thirties, Mary seemed intent that I become well acquainted with her divine Spouse, the Holy Spirit. I believe she had a role in arranging an opportunity for me to experience the Holy Spirit anew. The fruit of that encounter ignited a deep prayer life — and joy.

The defining moment of interior transformation occurred in St. Peter's Square amidst a roaring crowd of half a million ardent believers. The Polish Pope's words profoundly struck me: "Whenever the Spirit intervenes, he leaves people astonished. He brings about events of amazing newness; he radically changes persons and history." It was May 30, 1998, the vigil of Pentecost, and Pope John Paul II had convened a meeting of ecclesial movements in Rome to celebrate Pentecost in the year dedicated to the Holy Spirit.

In his homily, the pope proclaimed, "Jesus said: 'I came to cast fire upon the earth; and would that it were already kindled!'" (Luke 12:39).... Today, from this upper room in St Peter's Square, a *great prayer* rises: Come, Holy Spirit, come and renew the face of the earth! Come with your seven gifts! Come, Spirit of Life, Spirit of Communion and Love! The Church and the world need you." I personalized it: "I need You!"

As the Pope was leaving after his homily, the popemobile rolled to a stop near where I was standing, and I was able to look into the Holy Father's eyes. In his warm, piercing gaze, I saw incarnate love; he radiated Christ. I thought, "My goodness, holiness is attractive!" as I fervently prayed, "Lord, make me a saint like him!" This prayer rose from my ardent desire to magnify Christ's *joyful* love.

I repeated the prayer *Veni Creator Spiritus*. Opening myself entirely to the Holy Spirit, I was profoundly changed, never to become lukewarm since. With the breath of the Spirit, prayer becomes like breathing. To appreciate fully that defining moment, allow me to share how desperately I needed transformation.

Prayer of a Broken Heart

Two years prior to the 1998 Pentecost event in Rome, an extremely painful situation overwhelmed me with so much grief that I didn't want to live anymore. Initially, I didn't know how to react in a constructive way that would stop the hemorrhaging of the wound of my heart. I begged God to anchor me in Truth so I wouldn't succumb to the temptation that life isn't worth living.

Grace drew me to the Church's spiritual hospital: daily Mass. After Mass, I remained before the Blessed Sacrament. Jesus became my Divine Physician; the Eucharist, my medicine; prayer, my lifeline. Often I sat in silence, feeling only numbness. Then Christ's words broke through the darkness — words spoken to the ear of my heart: "Your life is a gift. You will not die of pain. You will arise and joyfully greet the light of a new day. Persevere in prayer, for I am with you always." Prayer is a path to divine encounter.

In Eucharistic encounters I learned the *healing* power of prayer for a broken heart. Over time, my heart was healed; joy and hope were restored. The grace of Rome's Pentecost event was not only transformative but also perfectly timed. That I was drawn to the Eucharist was grace but also memory.

An Interior Conversation

"When you talk to God, does He talk back to you?" As a child I made this inquiry to my mother as we strolled along the two-mile path from our home to the local parish. Routinely, my stay-at-home mom gathered her five young children to "visit Jesus," as she'd say. Upon arrival she'd position us in the front pew, and then she'd kneel at the altar rail before the Tabernacle. Because of her reverence, we naturally became silent before God's presence.

I stared at mom as she gazed intently—clearly she was silently communicating with Christ. I delighted to observe her in prayer, noting that a woman in prayer is a beautiful image. Mom deeply believed in the invisible God, and therefore so did I—almost by osmosis. "Of course Jesus talks back—a conversation takes two," was Mom's practical response to her inquiring daughter.

My mother's Eucharistic witness is etched in my heart. Her sacrificial life was very active, but prayer animated her maternal vocation. We didn't talk about prayer—we just prayed. Catholic education reinforced the practice of prayer.

In observing my parents' life and prayer, I learned that it's possible to balance work with prayer. St. Teresa of Calcutta advises, "We need to find God and He cannot be found in the noise and restlessness.... The more we receive in silent prayer, the more we can give in our *active* life."[4] Women who are contemplatives in action are great gifts to the Church and to the world because we mirror Mary's life.

THE MARIAN HEART PRAYS

In Mary and in my mother I perceived a connection between prayer and feminine beauty. Dostoyevsky reflected, "Beauty will

---

[4] Quoted in Richard H. Bell and Barbara L. Battin, *Seeds of the Spirit: Wisdom of the Twentieth Century* (Westminster: John Knox Press, 1995), 104, emphasis added.

save the world." I believe this. Whenever I see a mother loving her child, or a wife cherishing her husband, I perceive heavenly beauty. Through prayer, God beautifies the feminine heart. God speaks to our hearts in prayer, affirming our dignity.

From where does prayer arise? Let's look at what the *Catechism of the Catholic Church* says:

> Where does prayer come from? Whether prayer is expressed in words or gestures, it is the whole man who prays. But in naming the source of prayer, Scripture speaks sometimes of the soul or the spirit, but most often of the heart (more than a thousand times). According to Scripture, it is the *heart* that prays. If our heart is far from God, the words of prayer are in vain. (no. 2562)

Mary's is the unique feminine heart that prays in perfect docility with the Holy Trinity. Her heart can be considered a school of prayer. In fulfillment of Simeon's prophecy (Luke 2:34–35), seven swords of sorrow pierced her heart. Perhaps the pierced heart prays best.

PRAYER POWER IN THE PIERCED HEART

I previously shared how I learned the healing power of prayer for a broken heart. Consequently, I've been drawn to the *pierced hearts* of Jesus and Mary. Joseph Cardinal Ratzinger wrote, "In the pierced heart of the Crucified, God's own heart is opened up; here we see who God is and what he is like. Heaven is no longer locked up. God has stepped out of his hiddenness.[5]

---

[5] Joseph Cardinal Ratzinger, *The Spirit of the Liturgy*, trans. John Saward (San Francisco: Ignatius Press, 2000), 48.

Similarly, when our hearts are pierced, we are opened up; we face our poverty, step out of our hiddenness, and come before God with a hole in our heart. The Divine Physician attends to the wounded heart with tenderness. We remember that when Christ's heart was pierced at Calvary, water and blood came forth: new life (John 19:34)! When Mary's heart was pierced, Simeon says it was so "that thoughts out of many hearts may be revealed": revelation (Luke 2:35)! The pierced heart can be a portal of grace if we remain open to divine transformation.

What was the prayer of the pierced Immaculate Heart at Calvary? Mary's entire being resounded with *yes to the divine will*. No matter the cost, her gift of self to God was complete, steadfast in union with the yes of her Son, Jesus. Mary's yes at the Annunciation completely untied the knot of Eve's no. Our yes to God's plan has the power to heal and untie knots also. Mary's yes resounded at Calvary, affirming the yes of her Savior for the sake of the Resurrection. Our yes to God's plan is like the password that opens the treasury of heaven. "Yes, Lord" (*Dei voluntas fiat*) is Mary's prayer.

A WILLED, PRACTICED RESPONSE TO LOVE

Although a cradle Catholic, for a time in college and at the start of marriage, I ceased to pray. We must be honest and not deceived by excuses for not praying; I had many. After my reversion in 1991 (thanks to Mary's Rosary), I prioritized my prayer life.

Prayer lifts me out of myself, and circumstances, into the arms of God. I pray because I love God (who loved me first) and I cherish our relationship. But there is more to prayer. Romano Guardini teaches, "Anyone who takes his relationship with God seriously soon sees that prayer is not merely an expression of the inner life which will prevail on its own, but it is also a service to be performed in faith and obedience. Thus *it must be willed and practiced.*"[6]

For more than twenty-five years, my spiritual life has been centered on the Eucharist: daily Mass and holy hour. I've developed habits: Praying the Rosary (my favorite prayer!), I contemplate the scriptural mystery and incorporate the Ignatian practice of placing myself in the Scripture scene. I offer prayers of praise, gratitude, petition, and intercession spontaneously throughout the day, and I keep a prayer journal. There are days when I may not incorporate all of the above, but for the most part, I do.

To moms with small children—I didn't pray like this when my kids were young (regrettably). I know mothers with young families who strive heroically to prioritize their prayer lives inclusive of spouses and children. You are a great witness to the Church.

St. John Vianney encourages us, "Prayer is the source of all graces, the mother of virtues, the efficacious and universal way by which God wills that we should come to Him. Within the reach of the ignorant, enjoined to the simple and to the enlightened, prayer is the virtue of all mankind; it is the science of all the faithful! Everyone on earth who has the use of reason ought to love and pray to God."[7]

---

[6] Romano Guardini, *The Art of Praying: The Principles and Methods of Christian Prayer* (Manchester, New Hampshire: Sophia Institute Press), 4, emphasis added.

[7] Quoted in *Magnificat Year for Priests Companion* (New York: Magnificat, 2009), 28.

How Mary Prays: Scriptural Lessons

How did Mary's entire life become a living prayer? There are four occasions when Mary's words are recorded in the Bible. These words are keys to prayer, and we find them in the Gospels of Luke and John. Luke records the Virgin's dialogue with the angel at the Annunciation (Luke 1:26–38), her encounter with Elizabeth and her Magnificat (Luke 1:46–56), and the finding of the twelve-year-old Jesus in the Temple (Luke 2:41–52). John describes Mary's intervention at the wedding at Cana (John 2:1–11).

Mary speaks twice in her dialogue with the angel. In reply to his message, she asks: "How can this be, since I have no husband?" (Luke 1:34). Having received insight into God's plan, Mary gives her consent: "Behold, I am the handmaid of the Lord; let it be to me according to your word" (Luke 1:38).

+ Mary's request for clarity is the response of listening prayer.
+ Imbued with the Scriptures and a spirit of prayer, she surrenders in an act of obedient faith.
+ Mary's prayerful heart is docile to God's plan.

After her cousin Elizabeth greets her in Ain Kareem, Mary proclaims her Magnificat. She recounts God's intervention in her life and the fulfillment of God's promises made to Abraham.

+ Mary's prayer magnifies the Lord, not herself.
+ Her prayer is animated with praise and gratitude.
+ Her prayer is a remembrance God's covenant.
+ Her prayer is a proclamation of divine mercy.

We hear Mary's next words recorded in the Bible when the twelve-year-old Jesus is found in the Temple. His mother's words express distress: "Son, why have you treated us so? Behold, your father and I have been looking for you anxiously" (Luke 2:48).

+ Mary's questioning prayer is authentic.
+ She prayerfully surrenders to the mystery of her Son's response.
+ She ponders how she lost Jesus for three days and found Him. She will recall this during the three days before Easter.

The final time we find Mary's words in the Bible is in the fourth Gospel, when John narrates her involvement in Jesus' first miracle, at a wedding in Cana. Mary speaks twice. Turning to her Son she says, "They have no wine" (John 2:3).

+ Mary's heart of prayer is altruistic, sensitive to the needs of others.
+ Her prayer is intercessory, filled with expectant faith.
+ Trusting that Jesus would prevent the embarrassment of the couple and their family,
+ Mary tells the servants: "Do whatever he tells you" (John 2:5).
+ Mary's last recorded prayer instruction points to Christ.
+ Her prayer is detached but confident in God's mercy.

WITH MARY IN THE BATTLE OF PRAYER

Edith Stein, in an address just before Hitler's rise to power, urged a group of Catholic women: "Perhaps the moment has almost come for the Catholic women to stand with Mary and with the Church under the cross. It would be a shame to let her answer the call alone."[8] There's a call for women to pray with Mary at

---

[8] Laura Garcia, "Edith Stein—Convert, Nun, Martyr," Catholic Education Resource Center, http://www.catholiceducation.org/en/culture/catholic-contributions/edith-stein-convert-nun-martyr.html.

the Cross, especially now when many are running away from Christ in His suffering Body, the Church.

In Luke's Gospel we read, "Jesus turning to them said, 'Daughters of Jerusalem, do not weep for me, but weep for yourselves and for your children'" (Luke 23:28). Perhaps this is a calling not to sentimental tears but to tears of repentance, of reparation. Is He reminding women to accept His gentle love, and also to recognize the evil at hand and the need for conversion of life?

The Church looks to Mary and to her spiritual daughters, who, transformed by prayer, will lift up the Cross against the culture of death, sin, and evil. What can we do? Look to the parable of the ten virgins (Matt. 25:1–13). We must follow the example of the wise virgins and keep our lamps filled with oil. We must also be prepared for every godly work: the temporal and spiritual care of the human family.

At Calvary a great spiritual battle occurred between light and darkness, good and evil, life and death, truth and falsehood. Mary is wholeheartedly engaged. In allowing her Immaculate Heart to be seven times pierced, she becomes the woman who crushes the head of the ancient serpent. Mary is a prayer warrior, advancing God's kingdom.

Prayer, one of the greatest needs of the human family, is a battle that sanctifies:

The great figures of prayer of the Old Covenant before Christ, as well as the Mother of God, the saints, and he himself, all teach us this: prayer is a battle. Against whom? Against ourselves and against the wiles of the tempter who does all he can to turn man away from prayer, away from union with God. (CCC 2725)

Praying against Evil:
Spiritual Mothers

Marian spiritual maternity is at the heart of St. John Paul II's teaching on Catholic womanhood. St. Edith Stein explains:

> The intrinsic value of woman consists essentially in exceptional receptivity for God's work in the soul. For an understanding of our unique feminine nature, let us look to the pure love and spiritual maternity of Mary. This spiritual maternity is the core of a woman's soul. Wherever a woman functions authentically in this spirit of maternal pure love, Mary collaborates with her. This holds true whether the woman is married or single, professional or domestic or both, a Religious in the world or in the convent. Through this love, a woman is God's special weapon in His fight against evil.[9]

That woman is God's special weapon against evil is evident in God's plan to create Mary, the New Eve. The Virgin Mary is powerful in the defeat of evil, and her spiritual daughters are as well. We "overcome evil with good" (Rom. 12:21). Saints conquer evil, and prayer is a seed of sanctity.

For fifteen years I've served at the side of priest exorcists. Mother Mary often manifests *God-given* maternal weight in helping priests evict evil spirits. Once, when the priest exorcist called on Mary to "please step on the head of the serpent now," an imprint of a heel manifested on the cheek of the possessed person, and the demon left, screaming. Then the liberated person

---

[9] St. Edith Stein, *Essays on Woman* (Washington, DC: ICS Publications, 1996), 259.

affirmed that Mary's presence was effective. Women are called to bring Mary's presence wherever we may go.

On the spiritual motherhood of priests, Fr. Raniero Cantalamessa writes, "It is true that laypeople contribute to the support of the clergy, but their contribution to the kingdom and to the priests should not stop there. The Lord today is calling the faithful in ever-growing numbers to pray, to offer sacrifices, in order to have holy priests. A concern, a passion, for holy priests has spread as a sign of the times throughout today's Church."[10]

Prayer is an undeserved gift for the humble heart:

In prayer the soul is purified from sin, charity is nurtured, faith takes root, hope is strengthened, the spirit gladdened. In prayer the soul melts into tenderness, the heart is purified, the truth reveals itself, temptation is overcome, sadness is put to flight. In prayer, the senses are renewed, lukewarmness vanishes, failing virtue is reinvigorated, the rust of vices is scoured away; and in this exchange, there come forth living sparks, blazing desires of heaven, in which the flame of divine love burns.[11]

When women pray, grace forms us into *other Marys*. The desolation of the human family beckons women to pour forth, from their feminine hearts, the priceless oil of prayer (see Matt. 26:7). We can't give what we don't have. *Lord, teach us to pray.*

---

[10] Raniero Cantalamessa, O.F.M. Cap., *Sober Intoxication of the Spirit, Part Two: Born Again of Water and the Spirit* (Cincinnati: Servant Books, 2012), 60–61. Learn more about spiritual motherhood at the Foundation of Prayer for Priests (www.foundationforpriests.org).

[11] Jacques Philippe, *Thirsting for Prayer* (New Rochester, NY: Scepter, 2013), 2.

PONDER, PRACTICE, PRAY

+ How do you relate to Mary as the mirror and measure of your femininity?

+ How is the Holy Spirit leading your prayer life and helping you to hear God's voice? (see Rom. 8:26–27).

+ What is your greatest challenge or obstacle in the "battle of prayer"?

+ How are you living the vocation of spiritual motherhood of priests?

+ How is the Eucharist helping your prayer life to develop?

FEMININE WISDOM
Venerable Concepción Cabrera (Conchita)

Jesus, my Redeemer and my hope, you are the One who speaks to my heart with the language of love, with the unknown language of the Cross that contains so much joy. Because of my weakness and misery, humiliation is painful, obedience is heavy, recollection is sad, temptation is intolerable, suffering is disturbing, and any cross is tiresome. I am afraid to forgo my desires. And any kind of denial frightens me, but O my Jesus, I will be able to do all in union with you. Take away my coldness and give me the gift of prayer to listen to your voice that encourages me to give of myself for love of you. Speak to me always, Jesus, Infinite Goodness, and tell me, as you told the Samaritan woman, everything that I have done in order to move my heart to repentance![12]

---

[12] Conchita, *I AM: Eucharistic Meditations on the Gospel* (Staten Island, NY: Society of St. Paul, 2001), 20.

CHAPTER 2

The Transforming Power of Prayer

Johnnette Benkovic

My instruction as a child in the Catholic Faith came through the zealous tutelage of the Vincentian Sisters of Charity. Like most children of my era, our primary text was the *Baltimore Catechism*, a primer of Catholic teaching that posed a catechetical question followed by a concise, theologically accurate answer.

One question I remember was "Why did God make me?" The answer was characteristically simple and to the point: "God made me to know Him, to love Him, and to serve Him in this life, and to spend all eternity with Him in heaven." This short but profound statement sums up the purpose and substance of the Christian life. As the *Catechism of the Catholic Church* puts it, "The whole of the Christian life is a communion with each of the divine persons.... The ultimate end of the whole divine economy is the entry of God's creatures into the perfect unity of the Blessed Trinity" (nos. 259–260). How, then, do we come to

Adapted from *Experience Grace in Abundance, Ten Strategies for Your Spiritual Life* (Manchester, New Hampshire: Sophia Institute Press, 2016).

this relationship and union with God? As St. Teresa of Calcutta said, "Everything starts from prayer."

PRAYER AND THE CHRISTIAN LIFE

For the Christian who is serious about who he really is, prayer is not optional. As lungs are to physical life, prayer is to spiritual life. Without prayer, the spiritual life languishes, suffers, and dies. That is why Pope John Paul II reminds us, "Prayer is not one occupation among many, but is at the center of our life in Christ. It turns our attention away from ourselves and directs it to the Lord. Prayer fills the mind with truth and gives hope to the heart. Without a deep experience of prayer, growth in the moral life will be shallow."[13]

As the Holy Father's quotation suggests, prayer is not to be a sideline event or an activity reserved only for serious problems or Sunday mornings. As the gateway to divine intimacy, it is meant to be the "breath" of our existence.

The Holy Father suggests at least three effects of prayer. First, it informs: it "fills the mind with truth and gives hope to the heart." Second, it reforms: it "turns our attention away from ourselves and directs it to the Lord." Third, it transforms: it deepens our moral life by taking it from the shallowness of the sensate, to an increasing experience of the divine life. Through prayer our mind is renewed, our soul is purified, our heart is converted, and we radiate "the perfect unity of the Blessed Trinity." In short, we become conformed to the image and likeness of God.

---

[13] John Paul II, Address to the U.S. Bishops on their *ad limina* visit, September 21, 1993.

A MEETING WITH JESUS: JOHN 4:1–30

A story from Sacred Scripture dramatically illustrates the effects of prayer. Jesus is on His way to Galilee from Judea. Although there are two possible routes for the journey, Jesus chooses the one that takes Him through the Palestinian territory of Samaria.

Around noon the band reaches the outlying area of Sychar. They near a field by Jacob's well. Tired and hungry from their travel, they decide to stop for a while. The disciples head to the city to buy food, and Jesus sits beside the well to rest.

Soon He sees a Samaritan woman approaching the well. She carries a large water jug, and she is alone. This, coupled with the time of day, indicates something about her. It was customary for women to draw water in the morning and in the early evening, not in the middle of the day. It was also customary for them to arrive in groups, not singly. The fact that this woman comes to the well alone at noon suggests her story: she must be a social outcast, perhaps a woman of ill repute.

Perhaps the sight of a strange man sitting by the side of the well provokes caution in the woman. She can see by His clothes that He is a traveler. Is He safe? Why has He no vessel for drawing water? As she approaches, she can also see He is a Jew. What is a Jew doing in Sychar, a Samaritan city? What can be His purpose in coming there? Caution sweeps over her once more, but she needs the water, and this is her time to come to the well. Besides, her curiosity is piqued, and being no stranger to men, she draws nearer, arriving at the well to draw her day's supply.

Jesus is thirsty. "Give me a drink," He says to her. Now, this is stunning. In the first place, Jews had nothing to do with Samaritans. The strain was over religion. Jews considered Samaritans heretics and their women ritually impure. For a Jew to ask for a drink from any Samaritan was unheard of, but for a Jewish rabbi to ask for a drink from a Samaritan woman, especially one of questionable background, was shocking.

The woman expresses her astonishment: "How is it that you, a Jew, ask a drink of me, a woman of Samaria?" Jesus is quick to reply: "If you knew the gift of God, and who it is that is saying to you, 'Give me a drink,' you would have asked him, and he would have given you living water."

The woman is intrigued. What does this man mean by "living water"? Besides, He has nothing to use to draw the water out of the well. And so, perhaps with some sarcasm, she chides Him, "Are you greater than our father Jacob, who gave us the well, and drank from it himself, and his sons, and his cattle?"

Jesus' answer intrigues her even more: "Every one who drinks of this water will thirst again, but whoever drinks of the water that I shall give him will never thirst; the water that I shall give him will become in him a spring of water welling up to eternal life."

Jesus really has her interest now. Carrying the water jug to the well, drawing the water, and hauling the heavy full jug home again is hard work. Besides, her lonely trips are unpleasant reminders of her sinful state and poor reputation. "Sir, give me this water, that I may not thirst, nor come here to draw," the woman exclaims.

Jesus knows what she is thinking, and there is more He wants her to know, so He confronts her with her situation. "Go, call your husband, and come here," Jesus tells her. "I have no husband," the woman replies. Jesus says, "You are right in saying, 'I have no husband'; for you have had five husbands, and he whom you now have is not your husband; this you said truly."

The Samaritan woman is flabbergasted. Who is this man? How could He know all about her? Could He be anointed by God? "Sir, I perceive that you are a prophet," she replies and then continues with a comment that underscored their religious difference: "Our fathers worshiped on this mountain; and you say that in Jerusalem is the place where men ought to worship."

Hearing in her reply a desire to know more, Jesus tells the woman, "The hour is coming, and now is, when the true worshipers will worship the Father in spirit and truth, for such the Father seeks to worship him. God is spirit, and those who worship him must worship in spirit and truth."

"I know that the Messiah is coming (he who is called Christ); when he comes, he will show us all things," she replies. With this, Jesus reveals to her His identity: "I who speak to you am he."

Skepticism gives way to certainty! Doubt gives way to belief! Darkness gives way to light! The woman is overcome. There, sitting beside her at the well, is the Messiah, the Anointed One of God! Leaving her water jar behind, she runs off into the city to announce to all who will listen that she has met the Christ. "Come," she proclaims, "see a man who told me all that I ever did. Can this be the Christ?" And, following her, the people come out of the city to find Jesus.

INFORMED + REFORMED + TRANSFORMED = CONFORMED

On one level, the story of the Samaritan woman at the well appears simply to relate a chance conversation between Jesus and a woman He met while traveling from one city to another. No meeting with Jesus is ever by chance, however, and no conversation with Him is small talk.

In fact, many Scripture scholars say that Jesus intentionally chose the Samaritan route out of love for the Samaritan woman. He wanted her to experience the "living water" of the divine life, to be set free and drawn into union with Him. He went to Sychar in Samaria to save that which was lost.

Nor is the conversation between Jesus and the Samaritan woman coincidental. It is life changing and laden with eternal implications. Every word Jesus speaks to her carries a supernatural value that leads her closer to conversion and draws her to knowledge of God, to love of Him, to service to Him. Every word moves her along the continuum of transformation.

The first words Jesus speaks to the woman at the well are significant: "Give me a drink." Although Jesus is probably thirsty from traveling all morning, and while asking the woman for a drink also engaged her in conversation, Jesus' words indicate much more. He is, after all, the Second Person of the Blessed Trinity. And while He thirsts for water in His humanity, in His divinity He thirsts for something more.

These words remind us of another time when Jesus will acknowledge His thirst. Then, He will be hanging on a Cross, offering His life for us. In that moment, His thirst would spring from His infinite love for souls. And sitting at the side of Jacob's well in the little town of Sychar, Jesus thirsts for a soul. The conversation between Jesus and the Samaritan woman is one of conversion, a conversation that informs her, reforms her, and transforms her; a conversation that bids her to come into conformity with Him.

Although the woman is surprised that Jesus, a Jew, would ask her for a drink, she responds. Her response, questioning though it was, indicates an opening of her heart to Him. This is true of every conversion. God appeals to us; we respond to Him. He knocks; we open. "If today you hear His voice, harden not your hearts" (see Heb. 3:7–8). And when we open ourselves to Him, He enters in His fullness and gives us a share in His divine life. And it is this that Jesus offers the Samaritan woman.

But the woman is tentative. She has not yet grown in trust. She has not yet tasted the living water, the supernatural life He is offering her. She questions Him. How can He draw water with no bucket? Where can He get this living water? Does He think He is greater than Jacob, who gave them the well in the first place?

The woman wants answers before she is willing to trust, and she wants proof before she is willing to believe. She has not yet discovered what happens when God's invitations are embraced rather than excused. She has not yet learned that the invitation is pregnant with true peace and abiding happiness. This embrace would fulfill what all other embraces had promised but could not achieve.

Jesus is abundantly patient with her. He sees beyond her words into her heart. The fact that she remains in conversation with Him tells Him that she longs for the eternal life He holds out to her. And so He meets her questions with a greater explanation of the gift He is offering. He tells the Samaritan woman that the water He speaks of is a "spring of water gushing up to eternal life" (John 4:14, NRSV).

Gradually Jesus reveals to her the most profound of truths. He gives her light, a little at a time, so that her inner vision can adjust to the revelation and she will not be blinded by it. Jesus gently woos the Samaritan woman, tenderly drawing her to the wellspring of divine life.

And then the turning point comes. Captured by what Jesus offers, she expresses her belief in Him: "Sir, give me this water."

This is the step our Lord has waited for, and He takes the woman at her word. He asks her a question that bids her to confront her sin. Can she bear it? "Go, call your husband, and come here," Jesus says.

How her guilt must have burned within her! Even the water she has drawn could not quench the sting of reproach that sears her conscience. "I have no husband," she answers, and Jesus replies, "You are right in saying, 'I have no husband'; for you have had five husbands, and he whom you now have is not your husband; this you said truly."

There is something profoundly attractive about the truth. It reflects the light of God, a light that leads us into the Divine Mystery, regardless of our state or condition. It is a haunting light, this light of truth. It clings to us and holds us. It captivates us. It follows us and wrestles with us. It provokes our conscience and tries our soul. And, although we may wish to flee it, this light compels, and we are willing to go as far as the light will take us.

This is how truth enchants the soul and bids it to the heights, even as it plumbs the soul toward the unfathomable depths of its mystery. This is how Truth draws us to the truth about ourselves and enables us to surrender that truth to the mercy of God.

The Samaritan woman sees the Light of Truth. It radiates from the One who sits before her, for He Himself is that Truth. And this Light speaks to her beyond the light of her understanding. This Light speaks to her heart, to her soul. It helps her reach beyond her sin to grasp the incomprehensible — the pure light of God's love, a love that can re-form her and reshape her, that would transform her and make her new.

The woman knows this is no ordinary man beside whom she sits, and initially she finds the purity of the Light too much. She squirms in its effulgence and tries to divert the conversation, but the Light holds her fast, fascinating her with its beauty. And she remains engaged, basking in its purity.

Like a flower that opens its petals to receive the penetrating warmth of the sun, the woman has opened her soul. The Son has pierced her darkness, and the Spirit of Truth has entered in. She speaks words intuited by the Spirit of Truth, prophetic words that identify the One with whom she speaks. She identifies the purpose of His mission, a mission already being accomplished in her. "I know that the Messiah is coming (he who is called Christ); when he comes, he will show us all things." Jesus sees the Spirit is at work in her, and so He tells her Who He is: "I who speak to you am he."

Now, her mind understands what her spirit already knew. The One who sits with her is the Messiah, and the living water has risen up within her! She has been released from the fetters of her past, and freedom is hers! The fire of divine life has been ignited within her, and she must share this good news with others!

The Samaritan woman runs into town, leaving behind the water jar with its weight of sin and burden of guilt. She is transformed. No longer a wanton woman, she is now an evangelist proclaiming the Truth and leading others to the well of Divine Life.

A Metaphor for Prayer

Our Lord's encounter with the Samaritan woman at the well provides us with a metaphor for prayer. It reminds us that this dialogue is like no other: it informs us, reforms us, and transforms us. It heals and soothes, convicts and forgives, unbinds and sets free. It brings light to our understanding and illumination to our soul. It can do all this and more because this dialogue is conversation with God.

Each day, Jesus sits at the well of our heart, waiting for us to come and converse with Him. He has journeyed there, outside of time and space, to invite us to the "living water." He is there to save us and to redeem us. He wants to attract us to the Truth of who He is and to reveal to us the truth of who we are in Him. He desires to engage us, to captivate us, and gently to unfold the petals of our heart with tenderness and care. He wants to pierce our darkness with the light of His love. He desires to transform us.

This is what true prayer is all about. Prayer releases streams of grace into the dried and parched tributaries of our lives, imbuing all that we do, indeed all that we are, with the life of God Himself. Prayer takes the mundane—such as drawing water from a well—and makes it spectacular. It takes the traumatic—such as seeing the reality of our condition—and makes it life changing. It takes our pain and our sorrow—such as broken relationships and unhappy decisions—and gives them eternal value. It takes our suffering—such as rejection, betrayal, and misunderstanding—and fills it with joy. In the end, prayer takes us—weak as we are—and makes us instruments of light and truth by transforming us into the object of our desire—Christ Himself. And we are sent forth to share that Good News with others.

PONDER, PRACTICE, PRAY

+ What are the three effects of prayer, and in what ways have you experienced them in your spiritual life?

+ Jesus went into Sychar to "save that which was lost." What aspect of your being has been lost and now found by Christ? What have been the life-changing realities of His redemptive grace in your life?

+ Once set free through the love of God, the Samaritan woman seeks to set others free by proclaiming the Word of God. To what extent has your transformation in Christ led you to lead others to Him? Look for three opportunities to be an evangelizer today.

FEMININE WISDOM
St. Teresa of Ávila

Mental prayer in my opinion is nothing else than an intimate sharing between friends; it means taking time frequently to be alone with Him who we know loves us. The important thing is not to think much but to love much and so do that which best stirs you to love. Love is not great delight but desire to please God in everything.[14]

Have great confidence, for it is necessary not to hold back one's desires, but to believe in God that if we try we shall little by little, even though it may not be soon, reach the state the saints did with His help.[15]

---

[14] St. Teresa of Ávila, *The Book of Her Life* 8, 5.

[15] Ibid., 13, 2.

CHAPTER 3

The Sigh of the Heart

Ronda Chervin, Ph.D.

I was brought up in New York City by atheist parents who met in the Communist Party, become disaffected, and then became informers for Senator Joseph McCarthy. God was no more real to us than elves might have been to most of you.

My first prayer was suggested to me by my godfather-to-be, a professor at Fordham University. I was studying Catholic philosophy in a frantic attempt to find some truth that would keep me from despair.

"Why don't you kneel and say the skeptic's prayer?" Dr. Balduin Schwarz suggested to me one day.

"Huh? What's that?"

"God, if there is a God, save my soul, if I have a soul!"

This "skeptic's prayer" came to me during a tour of Europe. On the stop at Lourdes, France, the first answer to my prayer came without my realizing it. Mary began to intercede for me — first, by showing me the beauty of the candlelight procession of the pilgrims at the miraculous shrine of Lourdes. Shortly afterward, a picture of Jesus came alive with His eyes looking right at me!

All the lay Catholics who surrounded me at the time of my conversion in 1959 were Benedictine oblates who went to daily Mass and prayed parts of the Liturgy of the Hours in Latin. I had a book for Holy Mass with the Latin on one side and English on the other and the same for the Liturgy of the Hours. At first I didn't realize that receiving Jesus in Holy Communion was the highest prayer.

PRAYER PARTNERS: MARY AND THE HOLY SPIRIT

It was only in 1967 that I added the prayer of the Rosary. A friend told me that she made a deal with God that she would pray the beads every day if her Protestant husband came into the Church. The day after she made her pledge, her husband said he wanted to become a Catholic. Since I wanted my husband to become a Catholic also, I said I would make the same pact. "But isn't the Rosary long and boring?" I asked. "No," my friend said, "I pray it while my husband fills the gas tank of the car."

This was a far cry from the meditative Scriptural Rosary, but it was a start, and it wasn't long before our Mother in heaven gave me feelings of comfort praying those wonderful words on those little beads. Later I would write a book with Sister Mary Neill, O.P., called *Bringing the Mother with You: Healing Meditations on the Mysteries of the Rosary.* I wasn't consciously trying to form a feminine bond with Mother Mary, but I now see that the consolation of the Rosary was her motherly heart comforting me.

Ten years after my conversion, I knew only formal prayer, which I loved for its beauty and truth. But I had never prayed in my own words from my heart. When my godfather suggested that I try to pray from the heart for at least ten minutes a day, I didn't catch on well. But I muttered a few words while doing spiritual reading.

The big change in my prayer life came in 1969, when I was prayed over for the new release of the Holy Spirit (a personal Pentecost) and received charismatic gifts. I could hardly sleep for the joy that was in me. From then on, I wanted to talk all day to Jesus from my heart. My biggest new understanding from the charismatic gifts was that God was not only Truth, but also personal Love.

This was just before I started teaching philosophy at Loyola Marymount University, where there was a small charismatic prayer group that grew within a few years from about seven students and a priest to five hundred.

Praying to the Holy Spirit before each philosophy class led to a change in the way I taught for the next forty-eight years. I assumed that I would simply use the notes I had from graduate school and my favorite books on each philosophical subject, and possibly write occasional articles in academic journals.

Instead, the Holy Spirit led me to infuse prayer into the classroom, not just at the start and the end of each class, but as occasion arose. If a student mentioned being anxious about a sick relative and wondering how a God of love could let people suffer, I would stop the class and have us all pray for that person. Since the students didn't seem to like the books I assigned, I started writing ones I thought would fit their needs. Sixty books later, I am still at it!

The center and source of my prayer life has always been the Eucharist. Here is the metaphor I employed about the Eucharist in my first book, *The Church of Love*. When a woman and a man are in love, they want nothing more than to enter into each other's bodies. They would be just friends if they preferred "words" to the marital union. Nowadays, I sometimes urge elderly Catholics who have no obstacles to daily Mass that "if, as it were, Jesus wants to leap down from heaven to come into your body, shouldn't you be there?" The Eucharist is incarnational love. And after receiving Holy Communion I silently pray, "You are mine, and I am yours; melt me, mold me, fill me, use me, and be with me until the next Holy Mass."

SURPRISE IN PRAYER: A VISITATION

The next big change in my prayer came in 1976 in this manner. Some women devoted to Our Lady of Fatima asked me if I wanted to have the pilgrim statue of Mary in my home for a week.

"I'm not sure," I replied. "Most of my family isn't that devout."

"No one wants her for Christmas," sighed my friend.

"Oh, then, sure. Bring her!"

It was a busy day when the bell rang and three women came in carrying a small coffin-like box. Opening it and setting the replica of the famous statue of Our Lady of Fatima on a table, they took out booklets with prayers.

I groaned. I didn't really want to say a lot of prayers just then. We got to the sentence: "Mary, take my cold heart and put your Immaculate Heart into me instead." At that instance, a sudden rush of peace filled my soul. This peace lasted for two whole years!

Now, to understand how surprising this is, you have to know that I am a highly nervous, irritable woman who never experiences peace at all, much less abiding supernatural peace. Mary is the instrument of peace that I needed desperately.

The graces of Mary, the Church's greatest contemplative saint, flooded my soul, especially during the night. Bursts of love, interior visions, and words in the heart called interior locutions (not audible), became common. Even my prayers in response seemed inspired and came forth in sweet grateful words of love. After that spectacular two-year period, I lost the profound abiding peace but continued to experience beautiful graces in prayer for many years.

PRAYER IN TIME OF LOSS

The death of my young adult son to suicide was the heaviest cross I have ever carried. I immediately identified with Mary's grief as depicted in Michelangelo's *Pietà*. I also identified with the seven swords that pierced Mary's maternal heart.

I prayed and prayed for a sign that my son's soul was saved. I wrote a long account of his death, and also my husband's death only two years afterward, in a book titled *Weeping with Jesus: From Grief to Hope*.[16] At a healing conference, the Lord graciously gave me a sign, an answer to my inquiry about the salvation of my son. In my heart Jesus said, "Your son experienced his foretastes of heaven in his joys. The pain of his interior emotional sufferings was unbearable.... You will find him in my Sacred Heart." Christ comforts the maternal heart.

The death of my husband ushered in a period I called "the gray night of the soul." My experience was nothing as extreme as what St. Teresa of Calcutta went through in her dark night of faith. My prayer in the gray night of the soul was filled with

---

[16] Ronda Chervin, *Weeping with Jesus: From Grief to Hope* (St. Louis: En Route Books and Media, 2016), Enroutebooksandmedia.com.

aridity, but I was faithful to prayer without the warmth of con-solation. I persevered through the grayness that eventually gave way to the light of a new day. The feminine heart is resilient.

Prayer Life of Ronda, Dedicated Widow

I was fifty-seven when my husband died at the age of seventy-four. At first I thought I would easily find a second husband. When giving talks, I like to amuse my audience, many of whom are older women, by recounting that after twelve men rejected me, I decided to go for Jesus as a second Bridegroom! Another little quip: "It didn't occur to me that a devout man of seventy who had never married, probably didn't get married because he never met me!"

I thought I'd try to join a religious community under forma-tion to include widows, but several attempts indicated that this wasn't God's plan for me.

At that time there was talk of the Church reviving the con-secration of widows as a vocation. If you read the Acts of the Apostles and the letters of St. Paul with this in mind, you will discover that there is mention of the younger "drunken, gossipy widows" contrasted with the ones over the age of sixty who live only for Christ and the Church (see, e.g., 1 Tim. 5:9–13). As I write this chapter, the Vatican is about to issue a ritual and rule for such consecrated widows. Bishops all over the world have been assisting in the formation of widows who want to live a consecrated life, not necessarily in community, but in the way that consecrated virgins live in the world to transform it.

In the meantime, a spiritual director suggested that I call myself a "dedicated widow" with a rule similar to those in process for consecrated widows.

Here is the rule I have been living for the last eighteen years:

I have made and renewed a private promise never to remarry.

I try to live simply, and whatever money I have left after the necessities, I give to the poorest of the poor or to pro-life or other worthy apostolates.

I dress in simple blue clothing: jumpers or dresses with blue or white sweaters or blouses, in honor of Mary.

I attend daily Mass and go frequently to Confession. I pray the Rosary, the Chaplet of Divine Mercy, and the Liturgy of the Hours and meditate on spiritual readings each day.

I spend an hour in silent contemplative prayer, either in a church or at home.

I devote most of my time to apostolic endeavors such as writing, speaking, and teaching. I am not under strict obedience but I do follow the advice of my spiritual director.[17]

Before I made this private promise and started praying in this way, I thought that choosing Jesus as a second Bridegroom would cause me to be a little more faithful and ardent in prayer. Instead, I came to realize that having Jesus as a Bridegroom means living in a different spiritual mansion of the interior castle. How so?

In Catholic theology a spiritual consecration is described as loving God with an undivided heart. I was a married woman when I received the grace of a mystical exchange of heart. My life was walking hand in hand with my husband, who, by the way, became a Catholic many years into our marriage. After my promise to God as a dedicated widow I placed both my hands in the hands of Jesus Christ. Through prayer, I surrendered much

---

[17] For more about the way of life for dedicated widows, see www.rondachervin. com; click on "Options for Widows."

more to God. I no longer struggled with a codependent style grasping for human love. I abide now in the love of my divine Bridegroom.

THE FEMININE HEART IN PRAYER

Let me conclude with some overarching thoughts about feminine prayer. Catholic theologians generally agree that the soul itself is feminine in relationship to God whether the human person is female or male. This is largely because of the feminine capacity for receptivity of the things of God. This feminine dimension facilitates contemplative prayer. That is why, even with our busy lives, we should make time for contemplation, disposing ourselves for the grace that God desires to give.

My guess is that some of you women readers are like me — high-energy workaholics who have an unfortunate tendency to squeeze daily prayers into an agenda filled with lots of other items. Even if the prayers I say are beautiful, such as my daily Rosary, if I pray them very quickly to "get them done," this is not conducive to contemplation. Instead, I should treasure my quiet contemplative prayer time, making it a priority after daily Mass and work obligations. I should relax into deeper prayer. The Rosary, the Divine Mercy Chaplet, and spiritual reading can be part of my quiet prayer time. But I need to enunciate the prayers slowly enough so that their meaning sinks into my frenetic little soul! Otherwise, I adopt the more proverbial masculine, task-oriented way of doing things.

I find that, in the image of Mother Mary and the women saints, most of us Catholic women pray in a slightly more heartfelt way than most men of my acquaintance. Those men love very much images of prayer such as spiritual warfare. I like to fight the battle against the wiles of evil spirits every day with the methods of spiritual warfare taught me by mostly male mentors. On the other hand, I never want to be one-dimensional in prayer. I desire to make room in my life for the deep experience of contemplative prayer for which the feminine heart is made.

PONDER, PRACTICE, PRAY

I pray during the day using the following brief aspirations as suggested by spiritual directors.

+ *What cross can I help You carry, Jesus?* Is prayer widening my heart to Christ's intentions?

+ *Jesus, act in me, with me, and through me.* Through prayer is my union with Christ more consistent?

+ *Lord, grant me to see Your goodness in others.* Is prayer making me other-centered, able to see goodness in others?

+ *Lord, what are You trying to reveal to me in this moment?* Is prayer helping me to live well in the present moment?

+ *Depressed? Pray, "Jesus, I need You right now—so that I can keep going."* Do I immediately invite Jesus into my anxiety, depression, sadness, and grief and allow Him to lead me out of the darkness?

FEMININE WISDOM
St. Elizabeth of the Trinity

Prayer to the Trinity

O my God, Trinity whom I adore, help me to become utterly forgetful of myself so that I may establish myself in You, as changeless and calm as though my soul were already in eternity. Let nothing disturb my peace or draw me forth from You, O my unchanging God. At every moment may I penetrate more deeply into the depths of Your mystery. Give peace to my soul; make it Your heaven, Your cherished dwelling place, and the place of Your repose. Let me never leave You there alone, but keep me there, wholly attentive, wholly alert in my faith, wholly adoring and fully given up to Your creative action.[18]

---

[18] Fr. Charles Erlandson, *Give Us This Day*, vol. 1, *The Gospel of Matthew* (Tyler, TX: St. Bede Press, 2011), 129.

CHAPTER 4

Prayer with Sisters in Christ

Dr. Pia de Solenni

Because I grew up as the only girl in a family of boys, my notion of what it meant to have a sister was, shall we say, limited. To be honest, many of my experiences of sisters involved watching them fight over even the most ordinary matters; so I was generally grateful that I was sisterless.

In high school, I was on the debate and speech teams. The former routinely placed me in a mostly male environment with which I was quite comfortable, given my family experience. Still I had very little experience of being around other women. Then I went to college, where I lived in an all-women dormitory for four years. Even with the challenges of sharing closets and kitchens, it was nowhere near as bad as what I had anticipated. Despite the good friendships I had with women, I still had no experience of what it meant to have a sister. Or at least I thought I didn't.

Recently, I asked several women friends to pray for another woman who was in a very difficult situation. Their generosity moved me. Not only were these prayer warriors committed to spiritual sustenance, but they also wanted to provide a tangible witness of their support: quickly they proposed to send her a care package. As one of the women put it, "We want her to know that she has sisters in Christ who are praying for her." Keep in mind that they did not know this woman's identity, nor she theirs. When I picked up the care package, it contained various comfort items and several hundred dollars in gift cards, a welcome surprise for the recipient, who was touched by both their spiritual and material generosity.

My friends' response gave me a retrospect through which to understand my spiritual life. While I'm blessed to have male friends, both priests and laymen who are generous with their prayers, I realized that it is through my shared prayer life with many women friends that I've come to have a sense of what it is to have a sister *and* to be a sister to a woman.

And while every soul has an essentially feminine response to God, my experience suggests that there's something uniquely feminine, even maternal, about the way in which women pray.

In 2004, the Congregation for the Doctrine of the Faith published the document *On the Collaboration of Men and Women in the World*, in which Cardinal Ratzinger (the future Pope Benedict XVI) wrote that one aspect of the vocation of women is to model what it means to be the bride of Christ. After all, the Church is the bride, and Christ is the Bridegroom; so everyone in the Church, whether male or female, is invited to be the bride. Obviously, this presents a challenge for men, who all have vocations as fathers, including spiritual fathers, and some as husbands. Despite these fundamentally masculine roles, as members of the Church they are called to a feminine response to God. Such has been the longstanding tradition of the Catholic Church to refer to the soul in feminine terms and to describe union with God in terms of a mystical marriage.

MARY'S FOCUS ON GOD

The first chapter of Luke's Gospel introduces us to the Mother of God, in large part by contrasting her behavior with that of Zechariah. We see Zechariah greeted by the archangel Gabriel, who tells him that the prayer of him and his wife, Elizabeth, has been granted: they will have a son. Even though Zechariah and his wife had indeed prayed to be blessed with a child, Elizabeth was now beyond childbearing years, and so at first he refused to believe that their prayer had been answered. He asked the angel how it could be possible.

Many (if not all) of us look for signs that our prayers have been answered. And all too often, we refuse the obvious signs, even a messenger from God, as Zechariah did.

Luke then recounts how the same archangel appeared to Mary. Now, presumably she had not been asking God the Father to become the mother of His Son. In fact, Mary's Canticle (Luke 1:46–55) generally confirms this. Like Zechariah, she is told something that exceeds her imagination. In Zechariah's case, though, he couldn't imagine that his longstanding petition had been answered. Mary questions the angel in the same way, "How can this be?" Upon hearing his response, she gives her consent.

In her yes to Gabriel, Mary allows herself to be taken into something greater than herself. The incredulous person might see in her a woman who would buy anything—sand in the Sahara Desert, the Brooklyn Bridge, that one secret food that will take off all the belly fat, and so on.

But as we see salvation history unfold, Mary's example becomes our model. Would that we could say yes to the unimaginable things that God asks of us at times, not to mention the merely mundane. This woman stands in stark contrast to the man Zechariah, with whom most of us probably identify more readily than with Mary.

As Monica Migliorino Miller writes, "Woman confirms the goodness of creation. The freedom of man is manifested in Mary as she stands in for liberated mankind precisely as a woman."[19]

Almost as if to underscore this great drama, Gabriel gave Mary almost the same message he gave to Zechariah. He tells her that her cousin Elizabeth is pregnant. Mary responds not by *resting* and simply wrapping her head around what has just happened, but by *going* to visit her expectant cousin. She has embraced what has happened and acts *because* of it.

I've long relished this passage. It illustrates a beautiful synergy between the contemplative life and the active life, between prayer and the things that fill our busy lives.

To bring this back to the witness of my friends and many other women in my life, I see that when women pray, there's a certain strength. Maybe it's not a strength that the world recognizes, but it's a strength that we all experience and draw upon. I find it uniquely feminine in light of the response of the Mother of God to God Himself. In our busy lives we try to stay focused on God and keeping His presence in the middle of our activity, just as Mary did.

Hearts Anchored in Christ

Scripture offers us many examples of holy women. I'll focus briefly on two, who were also biological sisters — Martha and Mary — to develop further my thoughts on women as sisters in Christ. We

---

[19] Monica Migliorino Miller, *The Authority of Women in the Catholic Church* (Steubenville, OH: Emmaus Road, 2015), 152.

know that with their brother Lazarus, they were close friends of Jesus. When Jesus wanted to relax with friends, He went to them. They were so close that Martha even chided Jesus about her brother's death, going so far as to say that Lazarus would not have died had Jesus been there (John 11:21). (Only someone who's almost like family could lay on a guilt trip like that!)

And yet Martha manifests her faith in Jesus, her conviction that He is the Messiah, the Son of God. Perhaps we forget this deep faith when we read Luke 10:38–42, in which Jesus has come to their home and Martha gets upset that Mary is sitting at His feet, listening to Him, rather than helping her with the preparations, a predicament experienced in most households. When Jesus admonishes Martha, we see the apparent contrast between her activity and Mary's contemplation.

But another aspect of the passage can be highlighted. Martha says to Jesus: "Lord, do you not care that my sister has left me to serve alone? Tell her then to help me." Jesus responds to her, "Martha, Martha, you are anxious and troubled about many things; one thing is needful. Mary has chosen the good portion, which shall not be taken away from her."

Go back and read that carefully again. At any point do you see Jesus telling her to not be active? He's telling her to not be *anxious*. The better part that Mary has chosen is the peace that comes from being united with God.[20]

After the death of Jesus, when Mary meets the risen Christ (whom she first mistakes for a gardener), instead of resting with Him, she is sent by Him to tell the disciples that she has seen

---

[20] Cf. Fr. Gabriel of St. Mary Magdalen, OCD, *Divine Intimacy* (London: Baronius Press, 2015), no. 21.

Him and that He is going to the Father (John 20:1–18).[21] Because of this mandate that she fulfilled, St. Thomas Aquinas called her *the apostle to the apostles.*

In both episodes, something about Mary stayed the same: she was focused on the Lord. Whether sitting at His feet or witnessing His Resurrection, she was not anxious or troubled. Her heart was anchored in Him.

When Mary first discovers the empty tomb, she runs to tell Simon Peter, who comes back with her and another disciple. They, too, see the open tomb. They are in the same place where Mary stays and eventually encounters the risen Lord. For whatever, reason, Jesus chose not to appear to them, but to Mary. And He chose her to spread the word to them.

In both Mary the Mother of God and Mary Magdalene, we see an openness to receive a truth greater than themselves, greater than anything that anyone has ever imagined. And we see this also in Martha, who tells Jesus that she sees He is the Messiah, the Son of God. In all three women, we see how their belief and conviction shape their activity. In contrast with the apostles, who are closest to Jesus and overcome with fear at times, Scripture never indicates fear on the part of these women.

To my mind, there's no doubt that we see in the Gospels and in the Christian tradition the lived example of the gift of self, even in the fearful apostles, men with whom most of us would have probably identified more than with the women I've put forth.

---

[21] Some biblical scholars consider Mary of Bethany and Mary Magdalene the same person. See, for example, Brian Kelly, "St. Mary Magdalene Is the Same Mary, the Sister of Lazarus and Martha of Bethany," Catholicism.org, July 19, 2016.

THE SPIRITUAL SYMBOLISM OF THE BODY

While all women and men are called to the gift of self, I wonder how much the gift of self is shaped by our sexually differentiated bodies? Throughout conception, pregnancy, childbirth, and her children's early years, a woman's body gives of itself in a most concrete manner. From the very beginning of the child's existence, his mother sustains and nourishes him literally by giving (even if unwillingly) through her maternal body.

Insofar as every woman's body reflects this reality, whether she has become a biological mother or not, I see our bodies as formative of our psyches and our souls. After all, every soul comes to know *through* the sexually differentiated body with which it is united to create a specific human person. Each human soul *needs* its human body until parted by death. Until that point, that soul is informed through a specific body. It makes sense to me, therefore, that the female nature of my body would inform my soul in a specifically female way even though I've never been pregnant, much less given birth. And I would argue similarly that all women and men are influenced by their respective sexually differentiated bodies.

St. John Paul II wrote, "Perhaps more than men, women acknowledge the person, because they see persons with their hearts."[22] Could this not refer to the way in which a woman's body disposes her to see and interact with human life in its very beginning?

Don't get me wrong. I'm not trying to make generalizations about the sexes to suggest that all women are wonderful examples of humanity and men ... well, not so much. Rather, I'm trying

---

[22] St. John Paul II, *Letter to Women*, June 29, 1995, no. 12.

to get at a fundamental (and, I hope, complementary) way of looking at sexual differentiation, to the point that it affects even our spiritual lives.

Recall that earlier in this chapter, I cited Ratzinger, who stated that it was the vocation of women to witness what it means to be the bride, specifically the Bride of Christ.

BEING A SISTER IN CHRIST

For myself, I see that most clearly in my experience of prayer with other women. Whether I am offering prayer or am the recipient of prayer, there is a unique *feminine response*. Again, this is not to say that men don't respond quickly and effectively with prayer. The witness of countless saints, canonized or not, manifests that they can and do. Yet perhaps their response might be called feminine insofar as they model the Mother of God and many other holy women.

In my women friends, I see and learn from the example of Mary at Cana upon discovering that the wedding party has run out of wine. She doesn't go to her Son and say, "I think it's time to go home and get away from this noise." No, she goes to Him and points out the problem to Him: "They have no wine," as if she expects Him to do something about it. When He asks why it's His concern, she merely turns to the servers and says, "Do whatever he tells you" (John 2:1–10). Problem solved.

In the three women I've put forth for our brief reflection here, we see this perfect blend of the contemplative and the practical. They remain in the presence of God while also tending to the realities of the world.

On a most practical level, that's what I've learned from the prayer lives of so many women I know. A quick text message can launch a spiritual avalanche of prayer. And although I know men who respond in kind, I'd say that we women are gifted insofar as it might be easier for us to connect immediately with human need, since we are gifted with bodies that are disposed to the most vulnerable of human needs.

I see among women a more ready expression not only of the need for prayers but also of the response of prayers, prayers that don't disregard our basic human needs. This was what I saw in my friends who responded with prayers *and* a substantial care package. And I realized that I've learned from them how to be the sister in Christ that I grew up seeing in my mother: someone who spends countless hours praying through her ordinary work while also making sure that the person for whom she's praying also has other basic human needs taken care of.

Blessed Pope Paul VI closed the Second Vatican Council saying, "Women imbued with a spirit of the Gospel can do so much to aid humanity in not falling."[23] To my mind, these are the women we can all become when we pray as sisters in Christ, modeling our prayer after that of Mary, the Mother of God, bridging the gap between humanity and God as we unite our contemplative efforts to our very ordinary and practical day-to-day activities.

---

[23] The Council's Message to Women, December 8, 1965.

PONDER, PRACTICE, PRAY

+ How do you stay focused on God in the midst of your busy life?
+ Has praying with sisters in Christ been a blessing or a challenge? How so?
+ How has this chapter helped you to understand your feminine vocation and the power of prayer?
+ In what ways does your prayer life bless the broader Church?

FEMININE WISDOM
St. Faustina

A soul should be faithful to prayer despite torments, dryness, and temptations; because oftentimes the realization of God's great plans depends mainly on such prayer. If we do not persevere in such prayer, we frustrate what the Lord wanted to do through us or within us. Let every soul remember these words. And being in anguish, He prayed longer.[24]

Jesus to St. Faustina: "My child, life on earth is a struggle indeed; a great struggle for My kingdom. But fear not, because you are not alone. I am always supporting you, so lean on Me as you struggle, fearing nothing."[25]

---

[24] *Diary*, no. 872.
[25] Ibid., no. 1488.

CHAPTER 5

God's Overflowing Grace

Mary Healy, S.T.D.

What the Lord has taught me about prayer could be summed up in the cry of St. Thérèse of Lisieux on her deathbed: "All is grace!"

All is grace. Everything I am and have is a pure gift of God. Every prayer, every good deed, even the tiniest step taken in the right direction has not been a result of my effort but only because, as St. Paul said, "the grace of our Lord overflowed for me with the faith and love that are in Christ Jesus" (1 Tim. 1:14).

I didn't always understand this. As a teenager, I attended several youth retreats where I experienced the love of God for the first time. I was drawn to Christ and eager to grow spiritually and live my Catholic Faith to the full. What was missing, however, was a prayer life. I had no idea how to maintain a continuous daily relationship with the Lord. And without a prayer life, there was nothing to check my deep-rooted assumption that growth in holiness was all about self-striving.

Over the following years, as I strove, I experienced failures at least as often as success. I was influenced by a culture that put God and His will among the lowest of priorities. Instead of getting closer to God, it seemed I was only getting further away.

Gradually I became deeply discouraged, with an intense inner emptiness that I could feel even physically. But the Lord in His mercy intervened and began to show me that "what is impossible with men is possible with God" (Luke 18:27).

GREEN LOG ON THE FIRE

One of the first great graces of prayer that the Lord gave me occurred when I was a graduate student at Franciscan University of Steubenville. The campus ministry had organized an all-night vigil of Eucharistic Adoration in Christ the King Chapel (how many lives have been transformed in that chapel!), and I decided to stay the whole night. So I went and dutifully began to pray. I prayed the Rosary, very slowly … and then looked at my watch. I read Scripture for a while, then prayed another Rosary, very slowly … and then looked at my watch again. The time was passing at a snail's pace. I read from a prayer book. I prayed every prayer I could think of. I was starting to get sleepy. Finally, around 2:00 a.m. I realized I wasn't going to make it through the night. So I got up and walked out into the cold night air—and suddenly it hit me like a meteor: *The Lord was present in me!* The same risen Jesus who was on the altar was alive in my heart in a perceptible, even tangible way. The inner emptiness was gone, and from that moment on, it has never returned. Even though I don't always feel the Lord's presence in the same way I did that night, I know He is there.

I learned that night that a lot more goes on in prayer than we may perceive. Even when it seems that absolutely nothing is happening, even when I'm bored and distracted, as long as I keep praying, the Lord is at work, moving subterranean mountains. As St. John of the Cross observed, if you throw a green log on the fire, it may seem for a long time that nothing is happening. But inside, that log is getting dryer and dryer, hotter and hotter, until finally in one instant it will burst into flame.

BAPTISM IN THE HOLY SPIRIT

Around the same time as that chapel experience, the Lord gave me another great gift. I went through a Life in the Spirit Seminar and was prayed over for baptism in the Holy Spirit. Being "baptized in the Holy Spirit" is the phrase Jesus used for the divine gift He came to give us: the Holy Spirit poured into our hearts, transforming us from within (Acts 1:5; 2:4). The essence of this grace is the Holy Spirit's revelation to us of the unimaginable love of the Father and the glorious lordship of Jesus. It is a bubbling up of the wellspring of divine life that we were given through the sacraments of Baptism and Confirmation. It activates the charisms, which are supernatural gifts the Lord gives us for our mission to the world.

I experienced all this not immediately when I was prayed over, but gradually over the next couple of years. In the process, my spiritual life turned completely upside down. It went from my being in the driver's seat to the Lord's being in the driver's seat, with me coming along for the ride. It went from my trying to row upstream and getting almost nowhere to being carried along on the river of God's grace.

MY GRACE IS SUFFICIENT

A turning point occurred shortly after I graduated from Steubenville, when I was living in a house with several other young women. We were all seeking to grow in holiness together, but there were times of tension and conflict in our relationships. As time went on, the Lord used these struggles to expose deep areas of sin in my life. I began to see vices that I had no idea were there: selfishness, pride, judgmentalism, a critical spirit, jealousy, resentment.

My initial response was simply to try harder to love others. But the more I tried, the more I seemed incapable of changing the self-centered drives within me. The image I had had of myself as basically a very good person—kind, loving, generous, likable ... and humble—was collapsing. One day I shared this with a friend, and to my complete surprise, she said, "Mary, I think God has you exactly where He wants you to be." It was a moment of grace. All of a sudden I saw with crystal clarity that the Lord was fully aware of all my poverty—all my weakness and failure, all my inability to bring forth the spiritual fruit that He desired—and that it was no problem for Him at all! He loved me unconditionally, and His grace was superabundantly sufficient for me (2 Cor. 12:9). He was just waiting for me to come to Him in desperate need of that grace and to rely on His power instead of on my own paltry resources.

From that time on, things began to change, little by little. My housemates and I realized that Satan is always working hard to make members of the Body of Christ see each other as adversaries, so that he can divide and isolate us. We experienced firsthand the power of prayer to disarm and disable the strategies of the enemy. Every time we spotted his tactics, we got together to pray, to repent to each other if needed, to express forgiveness, and to take a stand together as sisters in Christ against Satan, "the accuser of our brethren" (Rev. 12:10). We found repentance to be not a burden but a gift that truly leads to joy, and we experienced Jesus' Cross and Resurrection as a real power at work in us, enabling us to die to sin and to live for God.

THE POWER OF PRAISE

Throughout this time I found one kind of prayer to be more life-changing than any other (in fact, I think it is the best-kept secret of the spiritual life): *the power of praise*. I first experienced this gift through "festivals of praise" at Franciscan University — gatherings where the students would spend hours doing nothing but praising and worshipping God, lifting up their hands and singing their hearts out to the Lord. Since then, praise has been the foundation of my prayer life. Many Catholics are not used to praising God, except when singing hymns in church, yet praise is at the heart of both Jewish and Christian tradition. In fact, to praise God is to become who we really are, since we were created to live for the praise of God's glory (Eph. 1:12).

Our Lady teaches us through her song of praise, the Magnificat (Luke 1:46–55). She exclaims, "My soul magnifies the Lord, and my spirit rejoices in God my Savior." Her word choice may seem surprising, since the verb "magnify" means to "make greater." How can anyone make God greater, when He is already infinitely great?

What the Magnificat reveals is that as we praise God, He is magnified in our own hearts and understanding. We live in a world under deep oppression, where God is often pushed to the margins. To praise God is to break through that fog and enter the Truth Zone. We begin to see how awesome God is, how magnificent His plan is, how minuscule our problems are compared with His mighty power, how nothing is impossible for Him.

As we praise God, our spirits become awakened and alive to His love. Our minds become aligned with His purposes, and we begin to be aware of all that is possible and available to us from His throne of grace. Our weak little yes to God is enlarged to a much greater yes. Even more, praise affects the spiritual world. Evil spirits cannot bear to be present where God is being honored. Our praise makes demons flee.

Paradoxically, praise is the most powerful when you least feel like doing it. When it was still new to me, a friend and I got together for praise and worship. After a few minutes of praising and thanking God aloud, I was ready to quit. But she was still going full blast, so I kept going, even though it seemed a bit tedious and redundant. We continued for about twenty or thirty minutes, and, to my surprise, after a while the praise began to flow naturally, and I became more and more filled with the joy of the Lord. By the time we stopped, I felt an amazing lightness of spirit and clarity of mind. I could see everything from a more heavenly perspective, in light of the glorious kingship of Jesus in my life and in the world.

Our natural tendency is to praise God only when things are going well. But Scripture tells us, "Rejoice *always*, pray constantly, give thanks in *all* circumstances; for this is the will of God in Christ Jesus for you" (1 Thess. 5:16–18, emphasis added). I once experienced the potency of this injunction when I was at a low point. A combination of troubles in relationships and in ministry had really discouraged me, and everywhere I turned, there seemed to be insoluble problems. One particularly difficult day, as I was trying to pray, I felt like the psalmist who said, "The waters have come up to my neck. I sink in deep mire, where there is no foothold" (Ps. 69:1–2). I knew the Lord was calling me to praise Him right then and there, but there was nothing I wanted to do *less*. It felt as if it would be completely forced.

But as an act of faith, I began to thank God aloud—not *in spite of* my circumstances but *for* my circumstances. It was a way of acknowledging that He is utterly trustworthy and that He was caring for every detail of my life in His infinite goodness and wisdom. I smiled at the Lord and sang songs of praise. And as I did, it was as though clouds of darkness lifted and my whole disposition gradually changed. I *knew* I could trust the Lord, and that He would work all things together for good. I knew that I could have an unshakable peace and joy grounded in Him, not dependent on the ups and downs of my circumstances. The Lord was giving me "a garland instead of ashes, the oil of gladness instead of mourning, the mantle of praise instead of a faint spirit" (Isa. 61:3). And not long after that, the circumstances themselves began to change for the better.

To this day, I spend about two-thirds of my daily prayer time in praise and worship. I sing along with worship music, pray the psalms, pray in tongues, or simply praise God aloud. It is the best way to put off distractions, to enter the presence of God, and to open my heart to Him. As the psalm says, "Enter his gates with thanksgiving, and his courts with praise!" (Ps. 100:4). After praising God, the other forms of prayer—repentance, reading God's Word, interceding for others, or praying for my own needs—flow more from the leading of the Holy Spirit and less from my own limited human ideas. I'm able to pray with a heart more attuned to God's will and His wonderful purposes.

THE GIFT OF TONGUES

Closely related to praise is the gift of tongues, a kind of nonrational prayer of the heart in which we praise God aloud in an

unknown language (1 Cor. 14:2).[26] Praying in tongues is both
a prayer and a surrender, since you use your voice but allow
the Holy Spirit to form the words. St. Augustine speaks of it as
"jubilation": "a certain sound of joy without words: for it is the
voice of the soul poured forth in joy."[27] This gift was the very
first effect of the outpouring of the Holy Spirit on the Church
at Pentecost, when "they were all filled with the Holy Spirit and
began to speak in other tongues, as the Spirit gave them utter-
ance" (Acts 2:4). It has been rediscovered by many Christians
in our time.

I have found tongues to be a powerful means of intercession
as well as of praise. When I'm interceding for someone in need
and I'm not sure how to pray for them, I begin with tongues, and
then often the Holy Spirit will lead me to pray in a certain way.
"The Spirit helps us in our weakness; for we do not know how
to pray as we ought, but the Spirit himself intercedes for us with
sighs too deep for words" (Rom. 8:26–27). Throughout the day,
when I'm driving, or between classes, I often pray in tongues for
whatever people or situations the Spirit brings to mind.

---

[26] The gift of tongues is one of the supernatural gifts of the Holy Spirit
that St. Paul writes about to the Corinthians (see 1 Cor. 12, 13, and 14),
speaking of "the tongues of men and of angels" (1 Cor. 13:1).

St. Paul says he wants us "all to speak in tongues" (1 Cor. 14:5), although he earlier recognizes that not all believers do so (1 Cor. 13:30).

The Catechism of the Catholic Church teaches that the gift of tongues
is one of the special graces or "charisms" of the Holy Spirit: "Whatever their character—sometimes it is extraordinary, such as the gift of
miracles or of tongues—charisms are oriented toward sanctifying grace
and are intended for the common good of the Church" (CCC 2003).

[27] St. Augustine, On the Psalms 99, 3.

LECTIO DIVINA

When the Lord called the prophet Samuel as a boy, he was instructed to respond: "Speak, Lord, your servant is listening" (see 1 Sam. 3:9). I have to admit that my prayer often goes more like, "Listen, Lord, your servant is speaking." But prayer is a genuine conversation only if it includes truly listening to the Lord. And the best way to listen to Him is through Scripture, His living Word.

When I first began to study the Bible, I experienced what the disciples on the road to Emmaus felt: "Did not our hearts burn within us while he talked to us on the road, while he opened to us the scriptures?" (Luke 24:32). Gradually I formed a daily habit of lectio divina, which simply means reading Scripture in conversation with God. Traditionally there are four simple steps: reading, meditation, prayer, and contemplation. You *read* a passage of Scripture slowly, paying attention to each word. You *meditate* on it, especially on any words or phrases that the Holy Spirit spotlights for you, using your mind to think about it and, especially for Gospel passages, using your imagination to picture the scene. You *pray* to God, talking to Him about what you're reading and asking Him for deeper understanding. And finally you *contemplate*, letting your mind rest and simply enjoying the presence of God.

Through daily lectio divina I experience the Lord renewing my mind. Scripture is inexhaustible, and even after reading the same passage for the hundredth time, the Holy Spirit may reveal something new about it. St. Augustine wrote, "How amazing is the profundity of your words.... How amazing their profundity, O my God, how amazingly deep they are!"[28]

---

[28] St. Augustine, *Confessions* 12, 14, 17.

DEEP CALLS TO DEEP

When I wake up in the morning, I am not typically overflowing with godly thoughts and heavenly charity. In fact, I need to be reconverted every day. I may wake up distracted, or grumpy, burdened with the concerns of the day, with my mind on worldly things, not at all attuned to God. I need time with the Lord to be brought back to the Truth Zone. I need to be immersed once again in His love so that I can walk through the day in communion with Him. That is why early morning is the best time to pray. "Awake, my soul! Awake, O harp and lyre! I will awake the dawn!" (Ps. 57:8).

And each morning, whether I feel it or not, God is there with a far greater desire to lavish His grace on me than my desire to receive it. "Deep calls to deep" (Ps. 42:7) — He is there inviting me to enter in, receive, partake, and enjoy the fullness of life He has for me. He invites you, too, to come to Him every day in prayer, so that He can "strengthen you with power through his Spirit in your inner being ... that you may have strength to comprehend with all the holy ones what is the breadth and length and height and depth, and to know the love of Christ that surpasses knowledge, so that you may be filled with all the fullness of God" (Eph. 3:16–19).

PONDER, PRACTICE, PRAY

✦ A helpful way to bring praise into daily prayer is to read one of the psalms of praise (for instance, Psalm 8, 16, 47, 100, 111, or 145) and then write down all the reasons you can think of why God is worthy of your praise (for who He is) and your thanks (for what He has done for you). Then praise God on this basis for five to ten minutes at the beginning of your prayer time.

✦ To begin practicing lectio divina, read a passage from the Gospels and go through the four steps mentioned above: reading, meditation, prayer, contemplation. In the second step (meditation), picture the scene and imagine yourself there, observing what Jesus says and does. Then share your thoughts and reactions with Him in prayer.

✦ To deepen your relationship with God and open yourself to His grace, find a time to sit in peace and quiet, free from distractions, and ask one of these questions:

> *Heavenly Father, what do You think of when You think of me?*
>
> *Lord Jesus, what is on Your heart for me today?*
>
> *Holy Spirit, what do I need Your help for today?*

✦ Then write down in a prayer journal what you hear the Lord say.

FEMININE WISDOM

St. Thérèse of Lisieux

A Morning Prayer

O my God! I offer Thee all my actions of this day for the intentions and for the glory of the Sacred Heart of Jesus. I desire to sanctify every beat of my heart, my every thought, my simplest works, by uniting them to Its infinite merits; and I wish to make reparation for my sins by casting them into the furnace of Its Merciful Love. O my God! I ask of Thee for myself and for those whom I hold dear, the grace to fulfill perfectly Thy Holy Will, to accept for love of Thee the joys and sorrows of this passing life, so that we may one day be united together in heaven for all eternity.

CHAPTER 6

Praying with the Saints

Lisa M. Hendey

The first saint I ever met lived in the curio cabinet on Treebark Circle. That wooden abode was a place in our small suburban home that held the special treasures that we could look at but never touch. I would often approach her, whispering my special intentions on tippy toes as I peered through the glass that held her in a tiny circular golden box. More often than not, she answered my prayers. So I believed, despite my childlike ignorance, in her power as an intercessory friend. And when I coupled those prayers directed to the Little Flower—whose relic my parents reverenced faithfully—with a decade or two on my oversized, glow-in-the-dark rosary for the really big intentions, I more often than not saw results.

Imagine how silly I feel now about my youthful exuberance, my earliest attempts at prayer. How devoted I believed I was in turning not only to my patron saint but also to our Blessed Mother in times of need! To be honest, those "needs" were almost always purely selfish: that a best friend would be able to sleep over, that Santa would know that I really needed that new Barbie camper everyone else had, or that my pesky siblings would stop driving me crazy. I didn't have the theological words or formation to understand the concept of intercessory prayer. I knew only that my parents loved St. Thérèse enough to hold a "piece" of her (actually probably a minor, but blessed, third-class relic) in a place of great honor in our home. I knew that this beautiful young saint loved Jesus very much. And I trusted that in coupling my prayers to St. Thérèse of Lisieux with my prayers to our Lady, I would be well covered.

Having been born in 1963 and firmly catechized in the aftermath of Vatican II (that is to say, not very effectively catechized according to the older standards), I grew up in a beautiful Catholic home. I've always been able to understand and appreciate the concept of the domestic church, because I lived in one that fully lived out the teachings of *Lumen Gentium*:

> The family is, so to speak, the domestic church. In it parents should, by their word and example, be the first preachers of the faith to their children; they should encourage them in the vocation which is proper to each of them, fostering with special care vocation to a sacred state. (no. 11)

However closely my birth and baptism coincided with the 1964 promulgation of this Dogmatic Constitution on the Church, I doubt that my parents intentionally knew they were building their own *ecclesia domestica*. More likely, they were simply passing along the very same love for the Church and her teachings that they'd known in their own childhoods and homes. And while we didn't memorize the *Baltimore Catechism* in our Southern California tract house, we firmly knew in our hearts that God made us to show forth His goodness and to share with us His everlasting happiness in Heaven. We knew it was our greatest gift and responsibility in life to know, love, and serve God. That relic of St. Thérèse, other sacramentals (such as my favorite rosary), and most importantly the prayers that filled our home instilled in me a deep, abiding love for our Faith. And simple though it was, the prayer life that blossomed in me in those early years has flowered into a great need to listen intently for God's voice and to pour my heart out to Him in prayer each and every day.

FROM CHILDISH TO CHILDLIKE

My idyllic childhood included a beautiful education provided by parents who believed that the financial sacrifices they made to send me to Catholic elementary and high schools and on to the University of Notre Dame were worthwhile and important. My school years were filled with both active prayer and worship opportunities and with calls to serve others. As a teen, I assisted with liturgical music. My days at Notre Dame afforded the opportunity to receive the Eucharist daily and to pray in the company of my friends. My parents modeled Catholic social teaching by caring for the community around them and including us in those efforts to practice the works of mercy.

So in honesty, it wasn't until I graduated from college and landed in graduate school in Nashville, Tennessee, that I was truly "alone" for the first time in living out my Faith. I was a newlywed, deeply in love with my then non-Catholic spouse, residing in the uncomfortable environment where I was for the very first time not surrounded by Catholics. I went from daily Mass attendance with my friends to forcing myself to go to Sunday Mass in an anonymous-feeling parish. For the first time in life, getting myself to Church was solitary and felt like an ordeal. Gone was the joy of being an active part of the Liturgy. Gone were after-Mass chats about the homily or a deep desire to be near to the Eucharist. Gone was the support system that had made living out my Faith easy and fun.

I blame myself for these fallow years, but in truth I also now in a way appreciate having gone through them. As painful as they were, they have helped me to understand more distinctly and console friends who are experiencing their own "dark night of the soul." While I never doubted God's love for me in those young adult years, I doubted my need to be in daily conversation with God. I no longer lingered to hear the sound of God's voice in my life. I operated too often on "Lisa power," assuring myself that I was all I needed to solve the problems in my life.

In truth, in my efforts to be increasingly independent, my lack of communication with God was also mirrored in the way I communicated (or didn't) with my husband, Greg. As newlyweds, we were intimately in love, but we had so much to learn about truly sharing our hearts with one another. In my attempts to cope with the busyness of Greg's schedule as a medical student, I grew increasingly uncommunicative. I didn't want to bother Greg or cause him worry, so I internalized small anxieties rather than bog him down with them. Over time, my desire not to "bother" my devoted young husband became a resentment that he couldn't just "figure out" why I was anxious or upset, even though I had never told him what I was feeling.

I realize now that I played this same "mind game" with God in those years. Shouldn't God just know what was bothering me, why I was upset or frustrated? Did I really have to use words to speak to God?

In time, I would learn that the answer to my questions was yes. I would learn that pouring out my heart to my Creator was not childish but *childlike*, as Jesus called His followers to be (see Matt. 18:3; Mark 10:15; Luke 18:17).

Creating New Saints-in-the-Making

Interestingly, even though I lived externally as an active Catholic all my life, it wasn't really until the birth of my sons, Eric and Adam, that I realized for the first time what it meant to have a full and beautiful interior prayer life.

Being a mother for the first time evoked emotions that drove me (often literally) to my knees. My words of gratitude for the miracles of my sons or the beautiful way in which Greg grew immediately into his role as father became my own psalms of praise. My begging pleas, amid the barrage of dirty diapers and sleepless nights, for the skills to be a worthy mom formed my lamentations. I learned to whisper bedtime prayers, to lead family Grace before meals, and to model for my growing sons an active and sincere conversation with God. And since Greg joined us at the Eucharistic table seventeen years into our marriage, I have never stopped singing praise for God's bounty in our home.

Among other things I learned in forming our little domestic church was a deep and abiding love for the Communion of Saints. Selecting and teaching my sons about their special patrons took me back to my own childhood love of St. Thérèse of Lisieux. As my personal devotions developed into professional writing opportunities and increased study of these holy men and women, my passion for intercessory prayer through the saints flourished. As the *Catechism of the Catholic Church* says of this "cloud of witnesses":

> The witnesses who have preceded us into the kingdom [cf. Heb. 12:1], especially those whom the Church recognizes as saints, share in the living tradition of prayer by the example of their lives, the transmission of their writings,

and their prayer today. They contemplate God, praise him and constantly care for those whom they have left on earth. When they entered into the joy of their Master, they were "put in charge of many things" [cf. Matt. 25:21]. Their intercession is their most exalted service to God's plan. We can and should ask them to intercede for us and for the whole world. (no. 2683)

I learned alongside my sons that the saints were not only valiant role models whose lives should serve as examples for us. I also had—for the first time—words to help me theologically understand my childhood devotion to the saint who "lived" in my house on Treebark Circle. I heard our Church teaching me that not only could Thérèse intercede for me and our little family, but that there were countless other intercessors who could be called upon to carry our prayers to God.

As the Church teaches us, the saints are not the "silver bullet" wish-list granters that I supposed the Little Flower was in my childhood. More potently, these mere creatures are formally recognized by the Church for their sanctity and rightly invoked in our prayers. Over the years, I have been profoundly impacted by my own path toward being a member of this Communion of Saints. Imperfect and frail as I am, I dialogue daily with these spiritual friends to ask them to carry the yearnings of my soul to the God, who loves me without limit or condition.

Four Saintly Friends

Four saints have risen to the top of my "most frequently called" list. In sharing each of them briefly with you here, I invite you to consider your own "friends list" of saintly companions.

+ *St. Patrick*: The Apostle of Ireland is close to my
  heart because I descend from an Irish family and
  also from a family of Patricks. I am profoundly now
  devoted to Patrick for his own youthful conversion
  and for his work in fearlessly evangelizing a society
  greatly in need of God's love. I invoke him when I
  feel myself faltering in my ability to share my Faith
  lovingly with others.

+ *St. Kateri Tekakwitha*: The Lily of the Mohawks fell
  in love with Jesus in her youth, even venturing away
  from her home community to be able to live her devotion to her Faith more freely. Kateri lived a short
  but impactful life, fiercely committed to prayer. She
  constantly sought opportunities to teach others about
  her love for Jesus. Although she died at a young age
  and was a simple young woman, she consecrated her
  life to God in her own way. I call on Kateri when I
  need courage to counter the hurdles in my life.

+ *Saint Francis of Assisi*: Most commonly known today
  as a serenely robed figure surrounded by animals,
  Francis was actually a first-class prayer warrior in a
  society that was falling to pieces. After his own profound conversion, he left the riches of his youth behind (literally dropping the clothes on his back) and
  walked into a future committed to relying fully on
  God's grace and to rebuilding God's Church. I turn
  to Francis as I seek to be an instrument of peaceful
  conveyance of God's love to friends and family who
  often want no part of it. Francis reminds me to be
  bold and lovingly to pick up my own hammer to re-
  pair wrongs I see happening in the world around me.

+ *Saint Clare of Assisi*: When I was recently hired to write a children's book about Saint Clare, I approached the assignment thinking that this cloistered saint was a little boring. I couldn't have been more wrong in my assumptions. This young woman escaped the comforts of a lavish upbringing to give herself fully to God's service. In creating a community of female prayer warriors, Clare revolutionized not only her sisters' lives but a world greatly in need of heroines of faith. I turn to Clare often for her light when my own prayer life falters. She has taught me that perhaps the most saintly thing I do every day is fully commit myself to praying for my loved ones and for our world.

Everyday Prayers with the Saints

Every day, before my feet hit the floor, I whisper my own "Yes, Lord" in emulation of Mary's fiat. I will admit, though, that all too often, my prayer life is as haphazard and disjointed as my to-do list or the state of my closet. It's not always pretty.

But my very best days begin, end, and are sprinkled with opportunities to sit in adoration of God's immense blessings in my life. For me, morning prayer time has become an indispensable necessity. And the days when I think, "I'm too busy to pray this morning" are the days when I quickly realize that I most need to be on my knees.

Time devoted to morning prayer is a luxury that my now-emptying nest has afforded me in the last few years. As a creature of habit and also a devoted journaler, I have developed my own rituals that are portable enough to take with me on the road wherever my hectic schedule may situate me. I open with a Morning Offering and the Allegiance Prayer, formally dedicating my day to God. I break open the Word with a short reading and lectio divina based on the day's Gospel. I use a breviary app to pray Lauds, the Morning Prayer of the Liturgy of the Hours.

Every day, I close my morning prayer time and begin the active part of my day with a study of and "conversation" with the saint being celebrated on the universal Church's liturgical calendar. Reading about the saints this way each day and journaling about what I can learn from their lives has become my favorite part of morning prayer. Their stories, even those of the saints most distant from my own circumstances, never cease to provide me with ample inspiration for whatever I will face during my day. From the martyrs, I invoke conviction and courage. From the mystics, I beseech passion and wisdom. From those who were just "ordinary" folks like me called to live out extraordinarily lives of sanctity, I ask the grace and strength to give God my very best in whatever I'm called to that particular day.

I'm relatively certain that I will never be canonized a saint. But in my prayer life, every day, I have the opportunity to ask the saints and our Blessed Mother to carry me closer to God "now and at the hour of my death." I pray that one day I will meet all of my saintly companions, the canonized and the unknown, in the joy of God's eternal company. Until then, I will keep company with them for as long as God gives me the joy of walking my own path to Him.

PONDER, PRACTICE, PRAY

+ Learn about the special patron saints in your own life (those whose name you have or those associated with your work, your interests, or your needs) and begin to develop an intercessory relationship with them.

+ Endeavor to learn about a "new to you" saint each week. Pray about what you might learn from the life of this saint. Invite him or her to walk with you along your path to sanctity.

+ Adopt new patron saints for your family and invoke their protection and inspiration.

+ Choose at least one saint's feast day per month and "feast" in honor of that saint with a special novena, recipe, or cultural adventure.

FEMININE WISDOM
St. Clare of Assisi

Letter to a Religious Sister

Love with your whole heart God and Jesus, His Son, crucified for our sins, and never let his memory escape your mind; make yourself meditate continually on the mysteries of the Cross and the anguish of the mother standing beneath the Cross. Pray and be always vigilant. And the work that you began well, finish; and the ministry you assumed, fulfill in holy poverty and sincere humility. Do not fear, daughter, God is faithful in all His words and holy in all His works; He will pour out His blessing on you and your daughters; and He will be your helper and your best consoler. He is our redeemer and our eternal reward.

CHAPTER 7

A Heart-to-Heart with the Lord

Joan Lewis

> Now I lay me down to sleep.
> I pray the Lord my soul to keep;
> If I should die before I wake,
> I pray the Lord my soul to take. Amen.

This is the first prayer I remember ever saying. I'm not sure how old I was, but I remember learning this from my parents as they put me to bed at night. To be honest, I can't think of a time when prayer was *not* a part of my life. I was the oldest of four siblings, and my prayer memories include saying Grace before meals and reciting the family Rosary in May and in October, the month of the Rosary. Sunday Mass was always a family affair, and I remember having colorful prayer books when I was young and then beautiful missals when I was older.

Families always brought their children to Mass, and I'm sure that part of the time spent in prayer was praying that the kids would behave! I remember the Brennan family with thirteen children—everyone always at Mass. As children, we were taught that church was God's home and therefore a very special place, and Sunday Mass, the Eucharist, was God's big gift to us each week and therefore we must show our respect by being quiet or, in a word I learned later, by "recollecting."

Some families had babies, and they, of course, did what babies do: they cried, they were fed, and most then slept blissfully. Older children had prayer books with pictures, coloring books, and so forth. Everything was geared toward Mass. Sounds idyllic, right? In many ways, it was. Families were always together in church. Businesses were closed on Sundays, and that surely contributed to church attendance and to families praying together.

PRAYER FOUNDATION: FAMILY

One family tradition that we enjoyed was building the May altar. Mom and Dad helped, but it was we four children who built this altar to Mary, often using orange crates and any remnants of blue or white fabric that we could find. One of my mom's treasures, a beautiful porcelain bust of a praying Blessed Mother, was always the centerpiece, around which we placed small vases of flowers from our garden, and on occasion we "borrowed" lilacs from our neighbor, Mr. Emerson. And, of course, we prayed the Rosary here.

I well remember watching Bishop Fulton Sheen on television, when television was fairly new and not every home had one (believe it or not!). We were not thrilled that our playtime after dinner was interrupted, but five minutes into the program, we were riveted by Bishop Sheen, who always made us proud to be Catholic.

My prayer memories also include daily Mass during Lent with my dad. I loved going to morning Mass at St. Edmund's in Oak

Park, Illinois, and the special moments continued when we had breakfast at a diner just down the street. My prayer life today is linked to my dad in many ways, through his prayer books.

About six months after Dad died, Mom told me a wonderful story while I was helping her sort his things. Dad was the idea man, the project man, the builder and the repairman in the family. In fact, I have no recollection of a repairman ever entering our home as I was growing up because Dad could always fix what was broken. He often worked late into the night after dinner, fixing, adjusting, or inventing something in his special workshop.

One night, when things were quieter than usual, Mom went downstairs and found him not in his workshop, but in our den, reading one of the prayer books he had in his desk, one of many that he acquired over the years. The nightly talk they usually had in their bedroom to discuss family issues, raising children, finances, and the world's problems was held in Dad's office that night. They talked about faith, his books, and about how important it was to have quiet time to pray.

Mom gave me those books, and they have given me hours of joy over the years—the joy of inspirational reading and warm memories of a family in which prayer and faith were as natural as breathing.

Reflecting on my mother, I'd like to share Pope Francis's thoughts on motherhood spoken at the January 2015 General Audience when he dedicated the weekly catechesis to the family:

> A society without mothers would be a dehumanized society, for mothers are always, even in the worst moments, witnesses of tenderness, dedication and moral strength. They pass on the deepest sense of religious

practice — the first prayers, the first acts of devotion that a child learns.... Without mothers, not only would there be no new faithful, but the faith would lose a good part of its simple and profound warmth.

EUCHARISTIC DEVOTION

In my sophomore year at St. Mary's College in Notre Dame, Indiana, I lived in Regina Hall, a very small residence hall. We had our own chapel, and for that entire year I was the official sacristan, setting up the vestments and preparing the missal at night for the morning Mass; and readying the chalice, the wine, and the hosts in the morning. I had to know the liturgical seasons and the feast days to choose vestments of the right color and had to know Latin to prepare the Missal for the readings (the Epistle and Gospel), as this was immediately prior to Vatican Council II and the eventual novelty of Masses being said in the vernacular.

To this day, I remember how, with a sense of awe, I placed the unconsecrated hosts in the ciborium, knowing that the priest, with the power vested in him through ordination, would change them into the Body of Christ — as he would change wine into the Precious Blood. As a child I had learned what Transubstantiation meant — and each day in the chapel I felt so near to that miraculous act.

To this point I have intentionally focused on personal prayer memories and family. When you build a house, you want to start with the strongest possible foundation so that it will last. It seems true for our prayer life also. If a strong foundation for prayer is set within the family in the early years of life, aren't the chances better that one's prayer life will remain — even if storms come along and shake it up a bit?

OF PRAYER, SCHEDULES, AND PRIORITIES

When I entered the more secular world of work after college, with new schedules and more demands on my time, my prayer life dimished somewhat. However, it has never occurred to me, in my decades on this planet, not to go to Mass on Sundays, on holy days of obligation, on feasts, on solemnities, and during the Triduum. I never married or had a family, so I cannot speak to how a busy, multifaceted, time-consuming family life might impact prayer life. And that is probably where most of us struggle now with our time vis-à-vis prayer life—or should I say "juggle our time"? Trying to find time for daily Mass or trying to find a break in the work schedule to pray one decade of the Rosary can be challenging.

I work in Rome and do not have a car there, so I walk a great deal or use public transportation. Often the wait for a bus is long (they are notoriously late), so I have developed the habit of saying one or more Hail Marys as I wait—you know: don't curse the darkness; turn the lights on!

Years ago I had a *Life's Little Instruction Calendar* on my desk, and each day presented a saying that usually made you sit up and think or, at times, laugh out loud. One day, I read this: "When you wish there were more hours in a day, just remember you have the same number of hours as Thomas Jefferson, Michelangelo, Thomas Edison, and Mother Teresa."

Of course, that made me think: I really can plan, I can find time for a more structured prayer life. For most of us, prayer life is also a matter of time management: daily Mass (or at least attending Mass as often as possible), daily Rosary (even a decade or two at a time), and spiritual reading (even small amounts that likely will lead to larger amounts). Where there's a will, there's usually a way, even in the midst of crushing work or family schedules. For example, instead of reading e-mails, we can use our cell phone or tablet to read a breviary, a few pages from the Bible app, a few lines from the life of a saint, or an inspiring e-book we've downloaded.

Breakthrough in Prayer

At age forty-five, following a particularly traumatic experience that I got through because of faith, family, and friends, I wondered what was next in my life. Suddenly one day I spontaneously turned heavenward (because that's where we always think God is, even when He is next to us), and said, "Lord, my life from now on is in Your hands!"

Suddenly I felt a calm I had not felt in a long time, and in my mind's eye I saw Jesus make a thumbs-up gesture and say, "Yes! Finally!" In the ensuing days, my heart was more open to receiving; my mind was more open to listening to the Lord's voice. Before, I had been talking to the Lord and asking Him for favors, but now I was having conversations with Him. Nothing mystical, no booming voice coming out of the sky to speak to me — just talking to Jesus as a friend; the friend whom the nuns and priests and my parents had always told me about as a child.

The *Baltimore Catechism* teaches that "prayer is the lifting up of our minds and hearts to God, to adore Him, to thank Him for His benefits, to ask His forgiveness," and now I was trying to do this in earnest. My conversation with Jesus became a "new and improved" prayer after the age of forty-five. Talking to the Lord Jesus became my way of praying informally when I was not at Mass and could not offer formal prayer or pray the Rosary.

AUTHENTICITY IN PRAYER

What has worried me most about my prayer life is my inability to pray like the saints, popes, and mystics. I've often felt unworthy and unable to express my love for God after reading the soaring verses of the psalms or the love letters of saints such as Teresa of Ávila, Thérèse of Lisieux, Alphonsus Maria de Liguori, John Paul II, and many others.

On several occasions in Rome, I was blessed to be at Mass in John Paul II's private chapel. I will not live long enough to encounter another person who prayed like John Paul! He was always at prayer when we entered the chapel, and immediately we felt that he was unaware of our presence because he was *totally* aware of Christ's Presence. I sensed something mystical as I watched him pray. I could almost hear the conversation he was having with God or, quite likely, His Blessed Mother, whom he loved so much. Those images are seared in my soul!

Then I realized that I am not Teresa or Thérèse or John Paul or a psalmist, those to whom God had given greater graces. I am Joan, created in God's image and likeness and with my own gifts. Those gifts did not include soaring, powerful love phrases.

Perhaps my "gift" is being able to talk, and sometimes cry and laugh with childlike simplicity, with my friend Jesus. And I can do this always. In the Morning Offering, I give Him my "prayers, works, joys, and suffering."

One thing I always do is thank God after I pray. Not just with the phrase "Thank God" that so easily trips off the tongue. But a true, heartfelt "Thank You, Lord." Even before He answers my prayers, I thank Him. I find myself saying, "Thank You, Lord" dozens of times during the day. I thank God in the morning for giving me another day, for the sun that comes out after a tremendous storm, for the leaves that turn magical colors in the autumn, for being able to share a meal or a coffee with friends and colleagues, for finding a seat on a crowded bus, for learning some new and interesting fact, for being asked to help someone in need, for being able to offer up physical pain or discomfort, for completing a writing or project deadline, for the unexpected phone call or e-mail from an old friend, for making an especially delicious dinner with a new recipe. The more I do it, the easier and more natural it becomes—just like praying a Hail Mary at a bus stop in Rome!

PONDER, PRACTICE, PRAY

+ What family prayer traditions (if any) remain with you?
+ Is gratitude a vital part of your prayer?
+ Recall the example of Pope John Paul II's interior recollection. How is God calling you into deeper prayer?
+ What fruit are you experiencing through interior conversation (informal prayer) with Christ?
+ What breakthrough in prayer have you experienced?

FEMININE WISDOM
St. Teresa Benedicta of the Cross (Edith Stein)

To have divine love as its inner form, a woman's life must be a Eucharistic life. Only in daily, confidential relationship with the Lord in the tabernacle can one forget self, become free of all one's own wishes and pretensions, and have a heart open to all the needs and wants of others.

Whoever seeks to consult with the Eucharistic God in all her concerns, whoever lets herself be purified by the sanctifying power coming from the sacrifice at the altar, offering herself to the Lord in this sacrifice, whoever receives the Lord in her soul's innermost depth in Holy Communion cannot but be drawn ever more deeply and powerfully into the flow of divine life, incorporated into the Mystical Body of Christ, her heart converted to the likeness of the divine heart.

Something else is closely related to this. When we entrust all the troubles of our early existence confidently to the divine heart, we are relieved of them. Then our soul is free to participate in the divine life.... Therefore, the life of an authentic Catholic woman is also a liturgical life. Whoever prays together with the Church in spirit and in truth knows that her whole life must be formed by this life of prayer.[29]

[29] Edith Stein, *Essays on Woman*, in *The Collected Works of Edith Stein*, vol. 2 (Washington, DC: ICS Publications 1987), 55–56.

CHAPTER 8

Pope Benedict XVI and Women Who Pray in Love

Kathryn Jean Lopez

One autumn morning I was in the Washington, DC, offices of *National Review*, and the Vatican was on the line, calling for me—which doesn't happen every day. A priest from New Jersey was calling via Rome "on behalf of the Holy Father" to invite me to receive a message *for every woman in the world.*

Once I got the Whitney Houston song "I'm Every Woman" out of my head, imagining what a sometimes hostile social media might say about me representing the women of the world in any context, I was humbled, honored, and fascinated by the invitation.

Close to the opening Mass for the Year of Faith, Pope Benedict XVI had, as I understood it, the inspiration to reissue messages that Pope Paul VI had issued at the end of the Second Vatican Council to different populations—to artists, to laborers, to scientists ... *and to women.* Confession: I was only vaguely aware that the messages existed, which had to be the point. By reissuing the same letters verbatim, it was as if Pope Benedict XVI was saying: *You never really heard this because we never successfully communicated it.* And the messages are relevant now—even more than when they were first delivered.

The message to women begins:

> And now it is to you that we address ourselves, women of all states—girls, wives, mothers and widows, to you also, consecrated virgins and women living alone—you constitute half of the immense human family.... The hour is coming, in fact has come, when the vocation of woman is being achieved in its fullness, the hour in which woman acquires in the world an influence, an effect and a power never hitherto achieved. That is why, at this moment when the human race is under-going so deep a transformation; women impregnated with the spirit of the Gospel can do so much to aid mankind in not falling.[30]

Wow, I thought—if only we had taken that message to heart then. I wonder how much more life-giving we would be, as a Church, as a culture. I made it my daily mission to promote *transformation in Christ* as an antidote to the relativism that we're drowning in—the human manipulation of God and man that Pope Paul VI warned about.

A Life-Giving Gospel

The message from the Church to women continues:

> You women have always had as your lot the protection of the home, the love of beginnings and an understanding of cradles. You are present in the mystery of a life beginning.

---

[30] Paul VI, Address to women, December 8, 1965.

You offer consolation in the departure of death. Our technology runs the risk of becoming inhuman. Reconcile men with life and above all, we beseech you, watch carefully over the future of our race. Hold back the hand of man who, in a moment of folly, might attempt to destroy human civilization.

When I talk about this message, I always include this part, because inhumanity is the thing that we're choking on. John Paul II spoke of this "culture of death" in his 1995 encyclical *Evangelium Vitae* (*The Gospel of Life*), in which he proclaimed the value and dignity of each person. On the day he died, tributes flooded my inbox from people of all faiths, citing that encyclical. Whatever our faith, we women know in our hearts what we need to do: we must protect, nourish and love the most vulnerable. Prayer is foundational to carrying this out.

Prayer Leads to Service

I remember standing outside the Supreme Court Building one cold January morning in 2014, about a week before the annual March for Life protesting the *Roe v. Wade* decision. I was listening to Eleanor McCullen, a woman from Massachusetts, who was a plaintiff in a case about a buffer zone that restricted access to the front of abortion clinics in the Bay State. McCullen had made it her ministry to ensure that women going into — and even coming out of — Boston's main Planned Parenthood facility know there's someone who loves them and wants to help. She stands outside and simply says, "Good morning" with a warm, grandmotherly smile. Speaking to a gaggle of Court reporters, she called to mind our "better angels":

Yelling is counterproductive, and that's my message when I give courses on sidewalk counseling. Gentleness and love! You have to love people, and Americans love people. People ask, "How can you love the woman and man? You never knew them." What about all of those hurricanes and disasters? The Philippines and Katrina? What did our American people do? They got in planes, trains, and buses; they built houses for the people.... We are a caring country, but the sad part is, we take the life of our young in the womb. We help people, and that's all I'm trying to do—help someone that's desperate and abandoned.

Earlier she sounded like Mother Teresa on the courthouse steps:

I'm at peace with my message of love.... The unborn child is the most defenseless, most marginalized, the most fragile. In fact, the poorest of the poor is the child in the womb.

See how she loves! A fellow co-plaintiff, a Catholic priest who used to do sidewalk counseling as a seminarian, tells me that Eleanor sometimes launches into prayers that suggest little distance between her and the Trinity. God is magnified in her words and in her actions because she prays. When you are with Eleanor McCullen you encounter a woman impregnated with the gospel.

That message Pope Benedict handed me concludes with:

Women, you do know how to make truth sweet, tender and accessible; make it your task to bring the spirit of this council into institutions, schools, homes and daily life. Women of the entire universe, whether Christian or non-believing, you to whom life is entrusted at this grave moment in history, it is for you to save the peace of the world.

Referring to this section in my talks, I often say, "We are called to save the peace of the world. This is what the Catholic Church thinks of women! It is, perhaps, a best-kept secret."

KATHRYN LOOKS TO CATHERINE, CATHERINE, AND CATHERINE

What Pope Benedict XVI did that day seemed to be an exclamation point on a series of Wednesday talks he had delivered in 2010 on great women of prayer and action in the Church. I couldn't help but think I needed to pay attention since he had three talks on saints named Catherine (of Bologna, Genoa, and Siena).

About the prayers of St. Catherine of Siena he wrote:

Many put themselves at Catherine's service and above all considered it a privilege to receive spiritual guidance from her. They called her "mother" because, as her spiritual children, they drew spiritual nourishment from her. Today too the Church receives great benefit from the exercise of spiritual motherhood by so many women, lay and consecrated, who nourish souls with thoughts of God, who strengthen the people's faith and direct Christian life toward ever-loftier peaks.[31]

---

[31] Benedict XVI, General Audience, November 24, 2010.

Pope Benedict XVI wrote about St. Catherine of Bologna's
Seven Spiritual Weapons:

1. always to be careful and diligently strive to do good
2. to believe that alone we will never be able to do something truly good
3. to trust in God and, for love of him, never to fear in the battle against evil, either in the world or within ourselves
4. to meditate often on the events and words of the life of Jesus, and especially on his Passion and his death
5. to remember that we must die
6. to focus our minds firmly on memory of the goods of Heaven
7. to be familiar with Sacred Scripture, always cherishing it in our hearts so that it may give direction to all our thoughts and all our actions[32]

About St. Catherine of Genoa the Pope wrote:

With her life St. Catherine teaches us that the more we love God and enter into intimacy with him in prayer the more he makes himself known to us; setting our hearts on fire with his love.[33]

About St. Matilda of Hackeborn (sister of St. Gertrude the Great, to whom he also dedicated an audience) he said:

Matilda gave an emphasis in liturgical prayer to the canonical hours, to the celebrations of Holy Mass and,

---

[32] Benedict XVI, General Audience, December 10, 2010; Pope Benedict XVI, *Holy Women* (Huntington, IN: Our Sunday Visitor, 2011), 105.

[33] Benedict XVI, General Audience, January 12, 2011; Benedict XVI, *Holy Women*, 117.

especially, to Holy Communion. Here she was often rapt in ecstasy in profound intimacy with the Lord in his most ardent and sweetest Heart, carrying on a marvelous conversation in which she asked for inner illumination, while interceding in a special way for her community and her sisters.... The whole world, the Church, benefactors and sinners were present in her intimacy with God. For her, Heaven and earth were united.[34]

About Blessed Angela of Foligno, he said:

From conversion to mystic union with Christ Crucified, to the inexpressible! A very lofty journey, whose secret is constant prayer. "The more you pray," she said, "the more illumined you will be and the more profoundly and intensely you will see the supreme Good, the supremely good Being; the more profoundly and intensely you see him, the more you will love him; the more you love him the more he will delight you."[35]

And in talking about the famous Joan of Arc, who committed her life to "daily participation in Mass, frequent Confession and Communion and long periods of silent prayer before the Crucified One or the image of Our Lady," he gave hope to all of us who don't always have the answers:

Our Saint lived prayer in the form of a continuous dialogue with the Lord who also illuminated her dialogue with the judges and gave her peace and security. She asked him with trust: "Sweetest God, in honor of your

---

[34] Benedict XVI, General Audience, September 29, 2010.

[35] Benedict XVI, General Audience, October 13, 2010.

holy Passion, I ask you, if you love me, to show me how
I must answer these men of the Church."[36]

In the examples of these saintly women, we get a sense of
what feeds and nourishes and protects a truly Christian life. We
also see complementarity and collaboration at work—essential
for our lives and the life of the Church. It is spiritual motherhood
that all Christian women are called to, and the world needs.

ENCOUNTER

When Pope Francis visited my alma mater, the Catholic University of America, in Washington, DC, to canonize Junípero
Serra, founder of the California missions, he talked about how
we have become an *anesthetized* people. He often talks about the
Church as mother and as a field hospital. We're never going to
tend to the wounds in the hearts of men (and women) adequately
without women who are committed to loving, longing, healing
prayer. There's simply too much pain for human action alone.
And human action needs prayer cover.

In December of 2012, I was back at the Vatican. This time,
Pope Benedict was addressing a group of Catholic leaders from
the Americas. Anyone who was jetlagged woke up when he
urgently warned: If you're doing any kind of evangelization and
are not encountering Jesus in prayer daily, your plans aren't going
to be worth all that much. Encounter, encounter, encounter, he
emphasized, just months before Pope Francis would come on the
scene and use the word repeatedly.

---

[36] Benedict XVI, General Audience, January 26, 2011.

LOVINGLY ARMED FOR BATTLE

And then there was the most powerful day of Pope Francis's papacy, as far as I'm concerned. It was a June morning when the world woke up to one of the first images of the Pope Emeritus and Francis together. They were in the Vatican gardens, dedicating the Holy See to St. Michael and St. Joseph. What a clear message they communicated! The spiritual battle is real. The Enemy is at work, and we need to be on guard.

And from my autumnal experience with Pope Benedict XVI, I couldn't help but hear him say, with the eyes of a loving father who met mine that October: *Be mothers for priests, for men in marriage, for men who are losing or have lost their way, for men who have never had a fair start in life.* In a culture that is skeptical (at best) about prayer and that is so deep in desolation that confusion reigns, the work of prayer is critical.

A woman from Iraq was featured in a documentary about Christian refugees from Islamic State genocide. She was among those who had to flee their homes in Mosul overnight in June 2015, or face conversion or death. She and her family chose Christ. "Thank God for ISIS," she would go on to say, because, before she had made that choice, her faith was lukewarm.

Our Holy Fathers, past and present, call us out of lukewarm faith. Prayer is essential to faith. We must pray unceasingly. If you've got little ones under your feet, you might be on your knees a little less than a single woman in the city or a retired grandmother. Whoever you are, wherever you are, being at the foot in the Cross in love seems to be God's call for women of every nation. Only in prayerful union with the wounded we will ever be equipped to offer the healing remedy of Christ. Women are called to do no less than, "save the peace of the world."

I remember the first time I prayed in the shrine to Our Lady of Consolation in Carey, Ohio. Looking at our Blessed Mother with her Son in her arms, praying at the reliquary with so many women saints, I realized anew: when women pray, hearts are turned toward God. When women pray, "Do whatever he tells you" becomes plausible. When women pray, peace becomes real, wounds can be healed. When women pray, lives are saved.

WOMEN OF THE WORLD, UNITE IN PRAYER

When I pray, I feel the presence of some of these women I've mentioned—the saints whom Pope Benedict helped me to know better. It's often the events of the world that I cover as a writer, commentator, and editor that draw me deeper into prayer. The more I know about the human pain of the world, including the famous and influential people who are human like the rest of us, the more I realize that what is needed is the love made possible by prayer.

When I pray with the Holy Father—and I have had a few opportunities to do so with different popes—I feel the call we all have to help rebuild the Church and radiate the Heart of Christ, through cooperative, faithful loving service—that flows from prayer.

PONDER, PRACTICE, PRAY

+ Do you know the nearness of a woman saint, one whose life and prayer inspires and guides you?
+ The Church's message to women speaks of "women impregnated with the Gospel." How does your prayer life include the Gospels?
+ How do you include pro-life intentions in prayer?
+ How do you relate to the spiritual battle and to spiritual motherhood in prayer?
+ Is there a particular pope or papal document that has helped you to grow in your life of prayer?

FEMININE WISDOM
St. Catherine of Siena

From the Father

Know, dearest daughter, how, by humble, continual, and faithful prayer, the soul acquires, with time and perseverance, every virtue. Wherefore should she persevere and never abandon prayer, either through the illusion of the devil or her own fragility, that is to say, either on account of any thought or movement coming from her own body, or of the words of any creature. The devil often places himself upon the tongues of creatures, causing them to chatter nonsensically, with the purpose of preventing the prayer of the soul. All of this she should pass by, by means of the virtue of perseverance.[37]

---

[37] St. Catherine of Siena, *Dialogue* 9.

CHAPTER 9

A Relationship with the Living God

Marilyn Quirk

St. John Paul II has deeply inspired me. He stated that, "Prayer has greater value and spiritual fruit than the most intense activity, even apostolic activity itself. Prayer is the most urgent challenge."[38]

Prayer for me is having a personal relationship with the living God. I was blessed to have two holy grandmothers whose prayers and example led me to have a personal relationship with my Heavenly Father and His Son, Jesus, from an early age. It was an undeserved grace.

In that personal relationship, prayer was like breathing, and I became aware that I was never alone. Jesus was my best friend and confidant, always accompanying me in joy and sorrow. I learned the power of prayer at an early age. I prayed for my

---

[38] John Paul II, address to members of the Union of Superiors General, "Holy See Briefs," *Guardian*, December 15, 1978, 12, posted at Newspaper Archive of *Arkansas Catholic*, http://arc.stparchive.com/Archive/ARC/ARC12151978p12.php.

parents, whose marriage was very turbulent. I often wept over the suffering of others. I also learned the practice of offering up small sacrifices to God for various intentions.

In high school I felt a distinct call to dedicate my life to God. Although I was baptized Catholic and made my First Holy Communion, I was raised in the Episcopal Church. So, in counsel with my pastor, I decided to become a medical missionary for the Episcopal Church. While studying medicine I met a young man through whom I was introduced to a holy Catholic priest and to the Catholic Church. My life began to take a dramatic turn. I became a Catholic, and the young man and I were married and began our family.

Ten years later, the pleasures of life, riches, and worldly concerns began to choke off my former spiritual fervor. I still practiced the Catholic Faith and appeared to be a good Catholic in the eyes of others. Our children were in Catholic school and attended Sunday Mass, but Jesus was no longer the center of my heart. My focus turned to self and activities that interested me.

Prayer of Repentance: Response to a Personal Pentecost

A woman began inviting me to attend a prayer meeting, but I made excuses not to attend. After several weeks she wore me down, and I finally went. It was at this prayer meeting that God mightily intervened in my life.

Tears of remorse began to flood my soul as I was convicted of how far I had fallen away from the Lord. I was dead in sin, and by His favor I was saved. God, who is rich in mercy, rescued me and brought me to new life in Him. I went to Confession. Then I asked for prayer to receive the grace of baptism in the

Holy Spirit.[39] For me, that experience was what Pope John Paul II termed a personal encounter with the living God, an effusion of grace. I experienced the Holy Spirit in what I'd describe as a personal Pentecost. The love of God was poured into my heart. I desired to pray and to read the Scriptures, and the Sacraments took on profound meaning. Suddenly I had a whole new appreciation of being a *woman in Christ.*

Then I realized that my life needed to be reordered and that personal prayer was to be a priority. That meant that I needed to set my alarm clock one hour earlier. I asked the Lord to give me the grace to get up earlier, and He did. I thought of the passage in the Gospel of Mark when Jesus, rising very early before dawn, left and went out to a deserted place where he prayed (see Mark 1:35).

"JESUS, TEACH ME TO PRAY!"

I learned that everything flows from our union with Jesus. He is the vine, and we are the branches; apart from Him we can do nothing (see John 15:5). Just as we need food to sustain our bodies, so prayer is the life of our soul. If Jesus needed to commune with His Heavenly Father, how much more do we!

---

[39] "'Baptizing in the Holy Spirit' means regenerating humanity with the power of God's Spirit. That is what the Messiah does. As Isaiah had foretold (11:2; 42:1), the Spirit rests on him, filling his humanity with divine strength, from his Incarnation to the fullness of the resurrection after his death on the cross (cf. Jn 7:29; 14:26; 16:7, 8; 20:22; Lk 24:49). Having acquired this fullness, Jesus the Messiah can give the new baptism in the Spirit of whom he is full (cf. Jn 1:33; Acts 1:5)." "Catechesis by Pope John Paul II on the Holy Spirit," September 6, 1989, posted at Totus Tuus — Totus2Us, http://www.totus2us.com/.

When Women Pray

In reporting on Pope John Paul II's "secret to success" in his book *Witness to Hope*, George Weigel stated, "Prayer is his secret source of energy which he draws from to accomplish so many things and to do them so well in such a short period of time." The Polish Pope, now St. John Paul II, taught us many lessons on prayer:

+ Put out into the deep of prayer in order to put out into the deep of mission.
+ Mission that does not spring from contemplation is doomed to frustration and failure.
+ Contemplation must always give birth to mission — if not, it will wither.

The Popes have consistently called for us to evangelize, but this cannot be implemented without prayer. We need a personal encounter with Christ to be inflamed with His love in order that we may share it. We are called to pass the love of Christ to others, as did the Samaritan woman at the well (John 4:29–30).

> So the woman left her water jar, and went away into the city, and said to the people, "Come, see a man who told me all that I ever did. Can this be the Christ?" They went out of the city and were coming to him.

In reading the books of St. Teresa of Ávila, her *Life*, *The Way of Perfection*, and *The Interior Castle*, I have learned very much from this Doctor of the Church. Prayer is a gift that God wants to give us. We must ask Him, "Lord, teach us to pray" (Luke 11:1). St. Teresa teaches that we don't need to read volumes of books on prayer — we must just begin to pray. She tells us that we come to God on two wings of prayer — humility and faith. We should never be satisfied with a mediocre prayer life. We should strive to grow in prayer, or we will become lukewarm.

THE VIRGIN MARY, MY NOVICE MISTRESS

I would like to speak of our Lady, the Mother of Jesus, who has and continues to teach me about prayer. She is my role model, my novice mistress, so to speak. She is an unceasing example to me.

It is beautiful to reflect on the first chapter of Luke's Gospel, wherein we learn how the Virgin Mary was overshadowed by the Holy Spirit and miraculously impregnated with the Word of God. Then she "arose and went with haste" and traveled ninety-two miles to bring the Good News of salvation to her aged cousin Elizabeth, who was six months pregnant. At the moment of her greeting, Elizabeth and her child, John the Baptist, were filled with the Holy Spirit; and the child in Elizabeth's womb leaped for joy. The fruit of knowing Jesus through Mary is joy.

Pope John Paul II, referring to our Blessed Mother, said, "She is the privileged and sure way for an encounter with the Lord; it is she who prepares us to welcome His word and makes us persevering in prayer in the expectation of the Spirit who inflames our hearts and leads us to put out into the deep with courage, toward the goals that the Lord is indicating."[40]

Mary's role at the wedding feast of Cana (John 2:1–12) expresses much of what I believe is the call of women. At Cana, Mary is a woman who is sensitive to a need and brings it to Jesus: "They have no wine"—and He worked his first miracle. Mary continues to see our need, our depletion, if you will. She continues to ask Jesus for the miracle we need.

---

[40] John Paul II, letter to participants in the 24th National Conference of "Rinnovamento nello Spirito Santo," April 28, 2001, *ICCRS Newsletter* (July–August 2001): 2.

INTERCESSORY PRAYER: THE
PRESENT ROLE OF WOMEN

I believe that we, as women, consecrated to our Lady, have a special role in the Church today—to be intercessors for a "time such as this" (cf. Esther 4:14). Women have special sensitivity, an empathy and compassion for the needs of others. We are also tenacious and persevering, as is needed for effective intercession. Our world, as well as our Church, is in a crisis. It is a spiritual battle.

Six months before he became Pope, Cardinal Wojtyla gave a prophetic word on November 9, 1976, while in Philadelphia: "We are today before the final struggle between the Church and the Antichurch, between the Gospel and the Anti-Gospel. One thing that remains certain: the final victory belongs to God and that will happen, thanks to Mary the Woman of Genesis and of the Apocalypse who will fight at the head of the army of her sons and daughters against the forces of Satan and will crush the head of the serpent."

I believe that we may be entering into that hour, and we need to follow Our Lady into the spiritual battle—with the weapon of the Rosary. Pope John Paul II said, "The Rosary is an effective weapon against the evils affecting society."[41] We must pick up our weapon and pray ardently.

Jesus taught, "If two of you agree on earth about anything they ask, it will be done for them by my Father in heaven. For when two or three are gathered in my name, there I am in the midst of them" (Matt. 18:19–20). Over the course of forty years

---

[41] John Paul II, apostolic letter *Rosarium Virginis Mariae*, October 16, 2002, no. 2.

I have experienced the great power and blessings of praying with other women. This prayer has formed bonds of friendship and love in Christ that continue to sustain us through the years. The power of prayer in our women's network, *Magnificat, A Ministry to Catholic Women*, can be found throughout the United States and in many countries around the world.[42]

THE FRUIT OF PRAYER

I would like to share some thoughts on the fruit of prayer.

We experience fellowship: It is inconceivable how much God desires to commune with us. St. Augustine said that God thirsts that we may thirst for Him. In prayer we come to know Him and experience His personal love for us. Then we love Him in return. Once we have experienced the joy of fellowship with Him, nothing will be the same. We will only thirst for more.

Prayer is a personal divine appointment with the King of Kings. In fellowship with God we experience the intimacy of divine charity. Just as spouses and friends grow in love through time spent together, personal prayer aids us in the experience of God's love.

I have been abundantly blessed by attending daily Mass and Adoration (prolonged communion with the Eucharist). I believe that we are going to realize miracles through Eucharistic Adoration. In *Ecclesia de Eucharistia*, St. John Paul II wrote that Adoration of the Blessed Sacrament "is of inestimable

---

[42] Magnificat, A Ministry to Catholic Women, is an international private association of the faithful founded in 1981. Based on the Visitation Scene (Luke 1), the association has more than a hundred international chapters. See www.magnificat-ministry.org.

value for the life of the Church. . . . It is pleasant to spend time with Him, to be close to His breast like the beloved disciple (cf. John 13:25) and to feel the infinite love of His heart. . . . How can we not feel a renewed need to spend time in spiritual converse, in silent adoration, in heartfelt love, before Christ present in the Most Holy Sacrament? How often have I experienced this, and drawn from it strength, consolation, and support!" (no. 25).

He changes us: St. Paul wrote, "We all, with unveiled face, beholding the glory of the Lord, are being changed into his likeness from one degree of glory to another" (2 Cor. 3:18). The word *transform* in Greek is *metamorphoo*, from which we get the word *metamorphosis* — as in the process through which a caterpillar is changed into a butterfly. God changes us in His presence. Bad habits are gradually transformed and erased. More love for others comes into our hearts. Even our appearance can be altered as the Lord's light shines through us (see 2 Cor. 4:6).

I have realized that through prayer, God changes the desires of my heart. Looking back, I have seen how the direction of my life has changed. The things that I held important no longer attract me. When we say yes to God and dispose ourselves in prayer, grace transforms us — it's His work of salvation in us.

He teaches us: He renews our mind. "Do not be conformed to this world but be transformed by the renewal of your mind, that you may prove what is good and acceptable and perfect" (Rom. 12:2). God's word is alive and active with power to enlighten and conform our mind to His as we meditate upon the Scriptures. "The unfolding of thy words gives light; it imparts understanding to the simple" (Ps. 119:130). As we read God's word and reflect upon it, it is amazing how often a word or a passage will come alive with understanding and be a source of meditation for the day. The Bible is like no other book that we can pray with!

It is a blessing to meditate each day on the readings of the Liturgy, the living Word proclaimed throughout the universal Church. Along with the Bible, over many years, I have loved praying the Liturgy of the Hours. I am continually amazed at the rich wealth within the pages of this prayer of the Church.

He helps us to discern: In prayer we come to know the Good Shepherd's voice, which "leads me in paths of righteousness for his name's sake" (Ps 23:3). Very often, while in prayer, God inspires us to *do* or *not to do* certain things. We may be prompted to call or visit someone in need. We may receive help in discerning a decision. I remember after Hurricane Katrina when we were in "exile"—not knowing whether our home was destroyed or where we were to live. I was praying in an Adoration chapel and the clear words came to me, "My home is by your altars" (Ps. 84:4, NABRE). I was filled with peace and joy, knowing it did not matter as long as I was with Christ.

He strengthens us against temptations: When Jesus prayed in the Garden of Gethsemane prior to His Passion, He told His apostles, "Watch and pray that you may not enter into temptation; the spirit indeed is willing, but the flesh is weak" (Matt. 26:41). He was preparing them for the temptations and trials to come, but they did not understand. All of us are tempted, but prayer strengthens us to overcome temptations. In my life, prayer has made it easier for me to handle things with which I struggle. One example is the proper use of my tongue: to respond with kindness when spoken to unkindly, to avoid speaking too much or too little, and so forth. We will never be free of temptations, but God will always give us the grace to be ready for the trials that await us and to overcome them.

He uses our gifts: The work of intercessory prayer for others is powerful. Battles can be won, wars can be stopped, lives can be changed dramatically through conversions; vocations to the priesthood and religious life can increase; family life can be strengthened — all through prayer! Jesus said, "Ask, and it will be given you; seek, and you will find; knock, and it will be opened to you" (Matt. 7:7). He taught us to be persistent in prayer.

God has taught me that when we go to prayer we do not need to have long lists of intentions but need only have them written on our heart. The priests in the Old Testament wore a breastplate called an *ephod* on which all the names of the tribes of Israel were written as a reminder when they went to worship (see Exod. 29:5). This concept frees me to focus on God in prayer so that, like Mary of Bethany, I can anoint His Body, the Church with the oil of intercessory prayer.

I close my reflection with the prayer of Mary: "My soul proclaims the greatness of the Lord; and my spirit rejoices in God my Savior.... The Mighty One has done great things ... and holy is his name" (Luke 1:46–49).

PONDER, PRACTICE, PRAY

+ How has God brought you into fellowship through prayer?
+ How has God changed you through prayer?
+ How has God taught you through prayer?
+ How has God helped you to discern through prayer?
+ How has God strengthened you against temptations through prayer?
+ How has God used your gifts through prayer?

FEMININE WISDOM
Servant of God Lucia dos Santos (Fátima seer)

The Most Holy Virgin, in these last times in which we live, has given a new efficacy to the recitation of the rosary to such an extent that there is no problem, no matter how difficult it is, whether temporal or above all spiritual, in the personal life of each of us, of our families ... that cannot be solved by the rosary.... When lovers are together, they spend hours and hours repeating the same thing, "I love you!" What is missing in the people who think the rosary is monotonous is Love, and everything that is not done for love is worthless.[43]

---

[43] Lucia dos Santos quoted by Fr. Donald Calloway, *Champions of the Rosary* (Stockbridge, MA: Marian Press, 2016), 247.

CHAPTER 10

My Ear to His Heart

Vicki Thorn

This chapter's title speaks of my life as I matured in the practice of prayer and embraced the ministry of Project Rachel, the post-abortion healing ministry of the Church, which I founded more than thirty years ago. A self-destructive friend who had given one child up for adoption and aborted another inspired me. The friend said, "I can live with the adoption; I can't live with the abortion." The name Project Rachel was inspired by Scripture: "Rachel mourns her children, she refuses to be consoled because her children are no more" (see Jer. 31:15).

Some time ago I was preparing to speak at a Magnificat gathering, and I had been praying about what to share of my journey. I went to the powder room, and in the silence there I heard God say to me, "You were a strong-willed sheep who needed to have your leg broken!" Suddenly my life experiences came into new clarity. I was strong-willed and was convinced that my life would go as I had planned it. My prayer was, "My will be done!" I recognized that in times of confusion, fear, and pain, I was being molded into a new creation. In these times God was carrying me and allowing me to heal and grow closer to Him, changing my attitude to "Thy will be done!"

The traditional explanation of the good shepherd carrying the sheep on his shoulders is that when a sheep was headstrong and wouldn't stay close to the shepherd, he broke its leg and carried on it his shoulders until the leg healed. Then the sheep would not leave his side.

After I was enlightened about being the strong-willed sheep, I found an image of the Good Shepherd that spoke to my heart. His eyes look at us tenderly. He is carrying a black and white sheep on his shoulders, and the sheep's head rests against the Shepherd's face. I noted that the sheep cannot see the shepherd in that position, but he is in no danger and is tenderly cared for. The sheep's worldview is that of the Good Shepherd. I was changed by that realization. Suffering people often speak despairingly of not being able to see God in their pain. Now I understood why we don't see God in those moments; we are held closely in His tender care.

Brought to My Knees

During the early years of my married life, through the unfolding of the following events, I learned that I was in charge of nothing. My husband's father died, most of my aunts and uncles died, I experienced miscarriages, each of our first three children had life-threatening illnesses, and close friends experienced a divorce (and the day the divorce was final, the husband was killed in a motorcycle accident, leaving my dearest friend with two small sons, a farm, and a factory). We left behind family and friends in Minnesota for my husband to take a job in Milwaukee, and then we moved to Rome for a year with three small children, immediately following my mom's death. I learned that life is what happens while we make other plans. In such times we pray about the crisis of the moment.

The experience of the unexpected health issues with our children brought me to my knees. I have a vibrant memory of sitting alone in a hospital thirty miles from my parents and eight hours from our home, praying my Rosary and asking for our Lady's help and protection for the daughter they had just told me would be retarded due to a severe urinary tract infection. We were told to find a kidney surgeon upon returning home because there was a serious kidney problem. In a moment of deep distress as this unfolded, God led my husband and me to a new place in our spirituality through a dear priest friend.

Upon returning home and finding the proper surgeon, we asked Father to give our daughter the Anointing of the Sick. In the process he told us, that as parents, we have special gifts in praying for our children. We embraced his wisdom. Surgery was performed; my daughter's kidney was severely damaged due to a congenital blockage. The surgeon said the kidney functioned at only 5 percent, but he had left it in because some kidney function is better than none in an adult woman. One year later, the kidney was 100 percent normal. A medical expert said he couldn't explain it because kidneys do not regenerate, and there was no profound retardation, as we had been told. God answered our prayers; he hears the cry of the human heart.

Praying in Rome: Meeting Saints

When we moved to and lived in Rome immediately after my mother's death, I was overwhelmed. We were in a strange country with three small children. I was buried in grief over the death of my mother. I don't recall much about that time in terms of my prayer life; I was very numb. But I recall that I began reading the lives of the saints.

In my reading, I came upon an Italian Blessed who lived in the mid-1700s to early 1800s. She was the mother of seven with a husband who loved her dearly. They lived a simple, poor life, but she was graced with many spiritual gifts. I learned that her oldest daughter was named Sofia and her second daughter was named Marrucia. This stopped me dead in my tracks. My first daughter is named Sofia, and my second is named Marisia! So began a long relationship with Blessed Anna Maria Taigi. I am always touched when I visit the chapel wherein her body rests because she still wears her wedding ring.

Afterward, when a family member needed counsel, Blessed Anna Maria Taigi sent me the postulator for her cause — a priest here in the United States. That was not a coincidence. I believe we need to engage the Communion of Saints as spiritual companions and intercessors. Sometimes we forget how many saintly women have gone before us.

FOUNDING PROJECT RACHEL: GOD WRITES STRAIGHT WITH CROOKED LINES

As I think about God writing straight with crooked lines, I reflect on divine providence, which led my family to the right place to found a ministry of healing.

I insisted on attending a Catholic girls high school and told my father I would pay for it myself — which I did. There I met the friend whose abortion pain led me to found Project Rachel years later when God moved us to another place and led me to the job of Respect Life director for an archbishop who believed in the vision of Project Rachel. This made it possible for the ministry to be founded. It took seven years, but when it came together, it happened in six weeks!

The next day, the media carried the launch of Project Rachel around the world on the Feast of Our Lady of La Salette, the Consolation of Sinners. This was long before social media! Many significant things have happened on the feasts of our Lady.

I had prayed long and hard about this ministry. This waiting journey taught me about patience and God's perfect timing. I learned to keep praying even when things looked bleak. Over time, through prayer, I have grown to trust God's providence and timing. This is hard for many of us because it often seems that God has not heard us. We need to remind ourselves that God says *yes*, God says *no*, and God sometimes says *later*!

When I started Project Rachel, I was a young wife and mother with a bachelor's in psychology from the University of Minnesota. Later my credentials also included being a trauma counselor and a facilitator in bereavement loss and prenatal loss. I believed post-abortion healing ministry needed to offer anonymity, have a strong spiritual element, and include a psychotherapeutic component. Today Project Rachel is a diocesan-based ministry that includes a network of specially trained clergy, spiritual directors, and therapists who provide compassionate one-on-one care to people who struggle with the aftermath of abortion.

PRAYER OF CATHARSIS

Over time, my prayer life has changed. When I was young, it was mostly rote prayer. As the mother of six children, my prayer became more personal. I talked to God and the Blessed Mother whenever I could grab a moment. As I have grown older, while my favorite prayers are still the Memorare, the Hail Mary, the Anima Christi, the Peace Prayer of St. Francis, and the Rosary,

I do a great deal of spontaneous prayer, bringing the prayers of my heart directly to God.

I came upon a bit of wisdom years ago that I'd like to share with you. God says we are to be like little children before Him. I believe that is an invitation to speak to Him from our heart with childlike honesty. We may be angry with Him or confused. When my husband had a stroke a couple of years ago, I prayed from my heart with a multitude of questions about why; and would he recover, and what would life look like? I call this the *prayer of catharsis*. Through this prayer—perhaps best prayed while we are alone because it is best spoken aloud—we unload the burdens of our hearts. We can be honest before God. (The children I raised were very outspoken!)

In Scripture sometimes people complained. Job did not tell God that he enjoyed his boils and he'd like more. He complained! For true intimacy with God, we need to speak to Him of our longings and our pain, from our hearts. Genuine intimacy is our goal in prayer.

OF HEALING PRAYER AND MARY

I am more aware of the power of God when I am blessed to pray with someone for healing. When we returned from Rome, we felt the need to pray with other couples, and we started a prayer group. We all prayed from our hearts about the challenges we faced as couples and parents. This was a great gift to all the young couples involved, and we saw miracles; for example, two infertile couples were able to conceive.

Some say that faith is caught, not taught. My godmother, with whom I spent much time, was a woman of deep faith. She had statues of saints in her apartment and taught me about them. She took me to Benediction, and we prayed the Rosary. She showed me what a life of faith looked like. She bought me a statue of Our Lady of Lourdes when I was young, and it was always in my room. From childhood, I knew that the Blessed Mother was *my* mother. My parents were wounded people, but people of faith. It was the Blessed Mother who guided me through the years.

When it became clear that the ministry of Project Rachel was going to expand in ways I couldn't imagine, on retreat I made a deal with God. "I will do what You ask, if You promise that my children will not leave the Faith and will be blessed with good spouses." God kept His part of the deal.

PRAYER FOR WOUNDED WOMEN

With Project Rachel, I've come to appreciate Jesus' special relationship to wounded women. Often we carry our woundedness with us and hold God's mercy at arm's length because we feel unworthy, but we should not do this. I find that the prayer "Lord, I give you permission to heal me" is quite powerful.

Praying with the Gospel passages in which Jesus heals women can also be very fruitful. Jesus healed the woman with the hemorrhage (Matt. 9:20–22; how often we've carried our pain for years) and the woman at the well who recognized Him as the Messiah in the revelation of her life (John 4:1–42; truth heals). He healed the woman who washed his feet with her tears (Luke 7:36–50; she who loves much is forgiven much) and the woman caught in adultery (John 8:1–11; "Neither do I condemn you; go, and do not sin again").

I recommend keeping a prayer journal to record the Lord's word spoken to your heart.

In response to attending a Project Rachel retreat, in which most talks are given by post-abortive women, a lady offered this: "Project Rachel takes you out of the hell you've been living in and brings you in to God's plan for you. Our Faith is about reconciliation and forgiveness. We recognize that we sin and make mistakes. All we need to do is go to God to receive forgiveness."

In the founding of Project Rachel my life took turns I never imagined! I have been blessed to see how God heals his broken people. I have seen and lived the power of prayer—in my life and the lives of countless post-abortive women and men.

PRAYER IN SPIRITUAL WARFARE

I have contended with another spiritual reality. The devil is very active. Society speaks of social evil but rarely about personal evil. When we are living in God's plan we will experience spiritual mischief meant to discourage, distract, and derail us. We must remain rooted in prayer and ask others to pray for us also. The prayer of St. Michael is always a great help.

We need to be attentive to nurturing our relationship with God. He always holds us gently (even the strong-willed sheep), whether we feel it or not.

PONDER, PRACTICE, PRAY

+ In your relationship with God, where do you recognize that He has written straight with crooked lines?
+ Do you relate to the strong-willed sheep, and how has prayer made you docile to God's will?
+ When you cry out to God in pain, do you experience the power of prayer?
+ Do you engage people to pray with and for you as needed for healing and strength?
+ Is God calling you spiritually or physically to help women who suffer post-abortion pain?

FEMININE WISDOM
St. Gemma Galgani

Healing Prayer

My Jesus, I place all my sins before you. In my estimation they do not deserve pardon, but I ask you to close your eyes to my want of merit, and open them to your infinite merit. Since you willed to die for my sins, grant me forgiveness for all of them. Thus, I may no longer feel the burden of my sins, a burden that oppresses me beyond measure. Assist me, dear Jesus, for I desire to become good no matter what the cost. Take away, destroy, and utterly root out whatever you find in me that is contrary to your holy will. At the same time, dear Jesus, enlighten me so that I may walk in your holy light. Amen.

CHAPTER 11

Just Pray

Kelly Wahlquist

"Don't let me lose my joy."

I was forty-three years old, standing in my dark family room at 3:00 a.m. with tears streaming down my face. It was the first time I can remember *really* praying to the Holy Spirit. Circumstances had dragged my heart toward despair, yet in that bleakness in sheer desperation I threw open the window of my soul, turning for comfort to a Person I only vaguely knew. I cried out for God's mercy . . . and He responded with such generosity and compassion that my heart overflowed with gratitude. He restored my soul, comforting and protecting me when I felt most vulnerable, strengthening a gift He had placed in me before I had even known it was there.

When the nurses handed me, swaddled in a pink blanket, to my mother, one of them said to her, "Here's your little bundle of joy." As I grew, her words proved to be truer than she knew. From the moment I entered this world there was an uncontainable joy instilled in my heart.

Recently, my mom gave me a letter written by a sweet ninety-four-year-old French nun who had visited our family when I was four years old. Although she was nearly a century older than I, we were buddies. In the letter, Sr. Andrea thanked my parents for their hospitality and said, "The little Kelly was my joy. What a smart little one God has given you. You can be very proud of her, she is a treasure, bringing joy to all." Although her English was a bit broken, her message was clear. I still cherish her words.

God had indeed gifted me with joy, a beautiful fruit of the Holy Spirit. So it is no wonder that in the midst of my tailspin toward despair I begged the Holy Spirit, "Don't let me lose my joy." I had heard the Holy Spirit referred to as the *merciful Comforter*, and at that moment, in the dark night of my soul, I needed comfort.

Can you remember a time when you needed that same comfort, and cried out in the night? Did you know that it was the Holy Spirit who was listening, ever ready to wrap you in His comforting presence?

My prayer that night was simple. It was straightforward. It was heartfelt. And as I curled up on the couch, and rested in the comfort of the Spirit, it was answered. That's how I think prayer should be: simple, from the heart, and a place where we find rest.

When life ceases to make sense, when circumstances overwhelm and anxieties arise, remember that God has given us another source of unfailing comfort in the arms of the Blessed Mother, and in the gift of the Rosary. As we turn our minds from the uncertainties of our lives, and ponder the joyful mysteries of the salvation story, the familiar cadence of the prayers, like the soft lullaby of a mother in the ears of a fretful child, can calm and soothe our troubled hearts.

THE ANNUNCIATION: GOD ANNOUNCES HIS PRESENCE

"When I was a child, I spoke like a child, I thought like a child, I reasoned like a child" (1 Cor. 13:11).

Each and every prayer is initiated by God. As St. Augustine told us, "God thirsts that we might thirst for him." Imagine that! The Creator of the universe is thirsting for you, is constantly drawing you to Himself. When we respond to that invitation, speaking and listening to Him, we come to know Him intimately. Through our prayer an intimacy is built that speaks directly to our hearts, and from that intimate relationship flows a desire to know, love, and be with Him evermore. All we have to do is to be receptive to His invitation to relationship.

At the Annunciation, Mary was receptive to the invitation offered by God through Gabriel. I take great comfort in knowing that her response—in essence, her prayer—wasn't an elaborate, eloquently stated reply; it was a simple, heartfelt, humble "Behold, I am the handmaid of the Lord; let it be to me according to your word" (Luke 1:38).

As women, each of us has a beautiful gift of receptivity that helps us to continue this dance of spiritual engagement and intimacy. Yet often we find ourselves mired in self-doubt and distraction every time we try to "go deeper." The best way to counteract these temptations can be summed up in two words: just pray.

The first time I was invited to a Bible study, instantly I fell head over heels in love with the Word of God. I wanted to spend every waking moment with that which had captured my affection, so I devoted all my time to reading Sacred Scripture. The more I encountered God in His Word, the greater was my desire to know God in my heart. I wanted *more*. Above all I wanted to know how to pray, but I was often paralyzed by doubts, such as, "I'm not very good at this." Then one morning while struggling in prayer, in my heart, I heard the Lord softly say, "Just pray," and instantly I understood that I didn't have to pray like a deeply contemplative mystic; I just needed to pray.

I soon learned that as I prayed, God was patiently teaching me. It was okay that my prayer was simple. God didn't expect me to win a prayer marathon. He was delighted to hold my hand as I took baby steps. And He was constantly initiating the next step, because He knew that with each step I would grow closer to Him. All I had to do was be receptive to His prompting.

THE VISITATION: GOD ENFOLDS US IN THE ARMS OF FAMILY

"Entreat me not to leave you or to return from following you; for where you go I will go, and where you lodge I will lodge; your people shall be my people, and your God my God" (Ruth 1:16).

When I was thirteen, my Auntie Mary died of breast cancer. She spent the last days of her life in the home of her baby sister, Auntie Lani, being cared for by her loving family. The day she died, November 20, 1982, many relatives and friends had been to visit her throughout the day. But that evening she was surrounded by women who had been praying for and caring for her around the clock—her mother, her four sisters, her two daughters, her sisters-in-law, and me, her godchild and niece. (It could have been a scene out of the movie *Steel Magnolias*.)

That night is a bit of a blur; everything happened so quickly. But there was also a moment when time stood still. As I walked from the bedroom where my Auntie Mary had just died, I found Auntie Lani in the hallway. She was thirty-two years old and the beloved baby of the family. Without words, Lani hugged me—a hug that was as much a comfort as it was a cry to be comforted. Then she wiped my tears and said, "Mary was my godmother too." She paused and then said to me: "From today on, I will be your godmother, and you will be mine."

Instinctively Lani understood that losing Auntie Mary had left within each of our hearts a profound void that only a mother could fill. And so Lani generously offered herself to me. "I will be your spiritual mother, and I need a spiritual mom too. From this day forward, we will hold each other up in prayer. We will be there to support, encourage, love, and console one another."

In the hallway of that little rambler in Roseville, Minnesota, God blessed me with a glimpse of the Visitation of Mary and Elizabeth—a moment in which two women share in cheerful humility, leaning on one another, holding each other up with a wordless pledge to support one another on the journey, no matter how difficult the terrain ahead might be.

That cold November night, and every night since, my evening prayers have always included my Auntie Lani. I know hers include me, too—although her prayers today hold more power than mine. Lani died six years after her sister Mary, so I now have three strong spiritual mothers interceding for me—my two aunts and God's mom. Knowing how much I depend on the prayers of those special women has made me very dedicated in my prayers for my own godchildren and for all the young women God has placed in my life.

The Incarnation: God Touches Our Hearts When We Need Him Most

"For God so loved the world that he gave his only-begotten Son, that whoever believes in him should not perish but have eternal life" (John 3:16).

In his homily at his inaugural Mass, Pope Benedict said, "There is nothing more beautiful than to be surprised by the Gospel, by the encounter with Christ." I think about that quote often, as Scripture has become a part of my daily prayer, and daily I am in awe of the beautiful surprises God has for me each time I encounter Him in His Word.

One Sunday I was reading Psalm 51. It's a psalm I read frequently, and I had highlighted two of the verses in the text:

Fill me with joy and gladness;
    let the bones which thou hast broken rejoice....
Create in me a clean heart, O God,
    and put a new and right spirit within me. (vv. 8, 10)

On that Sunday, my eyes fell on the verse that was sandwiched between those two highlighted verses:

Hide thy face from my sins, and blot out all my iniquities. (v. 9)

I read it a few times slowly, then out loud, and as I meditated on the verse, the words *blot out* took hold of my thoughts. Why did David choose the word *blot*? When one thinks of the word *blot*, one immediately thinks of a stain. So why did he not say, "scrub out"? Or "soak for hours"?

And then it hit me: to God, our iniquities aren't stains that have set. We don't need to hide our "unseemly side" from God as we approach Him. We don't need to be afraid that He will reject us because the effects of sin have set and stained our hearts. God's bountiful mercy and love need merely touch our hearts, and our iniquities are blotted out. He doesn't rub the sin in deeper, making us too ashamed to approach Him; He doesn't just brush it off, minimizing sin's damaging effects. God touches our hearts and absorbs those sins before they set, as the Holy Spirit blows His healing breath on the damaged places of our hearts. Truly, there is no need to hide or to pretend. God knows what we need before we ask it.

God loves us so much that He sent His only-begotten Son to blot out every sin. Letting the reality of that soak into my heart fills me with an overwhelming gratitude and makes me long to spend time daily with Jesus in His Word. The more I read Scripture, meditate on the meaning, take it to prayer, and rest in His Word, the more His love lifts my spirit, and the more I live in the joy of His salvation.

The greatest blessings in my prayer life come from spending time daily encountering Jesus in the Scriptures. If you walk away from this chapter with only one nugget of wisdom, may it be this: make time each day to read, meditate on, and soak in the Word of God.

THE PRESENTATION: RECEIVING THE GIFT OF SUFFERING

"For me, prayer is a surge of the heart; it is a simple look turned toward heaven, it is a cry of recognition and of love, embracing both trial and joy" (St. Thérèse of Lisieux, The Story of a Soul).

As I was praying the Rosary one night with my seven-year-old son, he turned to me and said, "Mom, I don't get it. The old guy tells Mary a sword will pierce her heart, and this is a joyful mystery? What's so joyful about a sword to the heart? Ouch."

I can't tell you what my answer to him was. I'm sure I stumbled through some response that would appease my heart too. He caught me off guard, and with a good question. It wasn't until years later when I went through my own piercing of the heart that I learned of the joy that comes through suffering with Christ.

It can be difficult to pray when we are suffering. Often our first response is: "Why me?" And it can be hard to trust in God's plan when we don't understand. It is during these times that our prayer can (and should) emulate the prayers of our Blessed Mother.

We should ponder these things in our hearts—meaning, we can pray, "Lord, what does this mean in light of Your will for me?" When I find myself struggling in prayer because I cannot comprehend any reason for my suffering, I take courage in the fact that Mary stood at the foot of the Cross and still believed in God's plan of sheer goodness. These moments in my life are a perfect time for me to pray to our Lady and ask her to help me trust God's plan for my life, just as she trusted.

At the Presentation, there is joy in the fulfillment of the Jewish law as Mary and Joseph take their Son, along with their animal sacrifice, to the Temple, but there is a greater joy and a more extraordinary fulfillment ahead. Simeon's words foreshadow the sorrows that will be shared between Jesus and His Mother. But it is precisely in sharing in Christ's sufferings, that Mary shared in the fulfillment of the greatest possible joy—the joy of the Resurrection.

When we turn to Jesus in prayer amidst our suffering, we can be confident that we too will receive the greatest reward. One day we will see Him again, and our hearts will rejoice, and no one will take our joy from us (see John 16:22).

FINDING JESUS IN THE TEMPLE: THE JOY OF UNEXPECTED ENCOUNTER

"To fall in love with God is the greatest romance; to seek him the greatest adventure; to find him, the greatest human achievement" (St. Augustine of Hippo).

I once lost my iPhone for three hours, and I freaked out. I can't even fathom what Mary and Joseph experienced when they lost the Son of God for three days. I think the intensity of that experience is lost on us, because we know how the story ends—Jesus is found in the Temple, safe and sound. Had Mary known Jesus was in the Temple, losing Him would not have been one of her sorrows. How blessed we are always to know where Jesus is!

There are times in my prayer life when I hit dry spells and feel as though I can't find Jesus. It is precisely at times like this that I simply go to where I know Jesus to be. I take comfort in his presence in Adoration, in the sacraments, in Sacred Scripture, and most importantly, in the Eucharist.

Imagine the surge of emotions Mary experienced the moment she found Jesus. It must have been like waves of relief and joy, mixed with questions and a deep longing to understand, washing over her. There are days when I feel as though I have to overcome a plethora of obstacles even to make the time to pray, yet the moment I begin my prayer, the worries of the day fade and the peace of Christ begins to fill my heart. Even though my prayer may be entwined with questions and the desire to understand God's will for me at that moment, there is always a joy that bubbles up as a result of just spending time with Him in prayer.

In those times when I am struggling, I go to where I know Him to be ... even if I don't feel Him there. I take *great* comfort knowing that although I may not be able to find Him, He will always find me. He will always run to me with open arms to embrace my lost heart! All I need to do is ... just pray.

PONDER, PRACTICE, PRAY

+ Whenever you think, "I should pray" or "I should go to Adoration," remember that it is God who put that thought on your heart, and just do it.

+ Pray for the women who have led and continue to lead you in the Faith, and ask the Holy Spirit to guide you as you spiritually "mother" others.

+ Make lectio divina a daily habit. It will change your life!

+ Unite your sufferings to those of Christ. If you don't quite know what that means, ask the Holy Spirit to help you understand.

+ If ever you feel as if your prayer life is dry, or if ever you find yourself being dragged into despair, just go to where you know Jesus to be. Turn to Him in prayer, sit with Him in Adoration, meet Him in the sacraments, listen to Him in His Word, and, above all, become one with Him in the Eucharist.

FEMININE WISDOM
Julian of Norwich

Our Lord showed me our Lady, Saint Mary, to teach us this: that it was the wisdom and the truth in her, when she beheld her Maker, that enabled her to know him as so great, so holy, so mighty, and so good. His greatness and his nobleness overwhelmed her. She saw herself so little and low, so simple and poor compared to God that she was filled with humility. And so from this humble state she was lifted up to grace and all manner of virtues, and stands above all. This above all causes the soul to seem small in its own sight; to see and love its Maker. And this is what fills it with reverence and humility, and with generous love to our fellow-Christians. The seeking, with faith, hope, and love, pleases our Lord, and the finding pleases the soul and fills it with joy.[44]

---

[44] Quoted in Robert Llewelyn, *The Joy of the Saints* (Springfield, IL: Templegate Publishers, 1989), 343.

Appendices

The Relationship between Personal Prayer and Liturgical Prayer

Kathleen Beckman

Although personal prayer is the subject of this book, it is important also to mention the corresponding need for liturgical prayer. In an initial meeting with my first priest–spiritual director more than twenty-five years ago, I shared my ardent desire to grow in the spiritual life. He advised, "If you want to grow in prayer, let the Liturgy of the Church form and fashion your spiritual life." He encouraged me to be attentive to the liturgical rhythm of the Church's prayer. He suggested daily Mass and recommended a daily holy hour before the Blessed Sacrament.

I took his advice to heart. For me, the spiritual life would be all or nothing. Daily Mass and holy hour were challenging at first. Then, like all good habits, they became a beautiful part of my daily routine. I believe it has been the greatest grace for growth in prayer. It anchors me in the praying Church.

Today, we are aware of people whose personal prayer life becomes so focused on the "I" that they walk away from the Church altogether. Personal prayer is the flowering of liturgical prayer.

In his *Art of Praying* Romano Guardini distinguishes between liturgical prayer and personal prayer.

Personal prayer is said in silence by the heart or spoken by the mouth and is accompanied only by the merest hint of gesture or action. The Liturgy, on the other hand, is above all a system of actions, of which prayer constitutes only one element.

Personal prayer and the Liturgy are the two main spheres of religious life, each having its own roots and character and each its unique significance. In personal prayer man is alone with God and himself. The Liturgy, however, is a united prayer of the Christian community. In the Liturgy it is not *I* but *we*; and the *we* does not merely signify that many individuals are congregated. It is not a sum of individuals but a wholeness: the Church.

It exists even when one or the other, or many, have divorced themselves from its body, for it does not have its origin in the desire of the individual for the community but in the creative will of God, which embraces the whole of mankind. It was founded by Christ, came into being on the day of Pentecost, and will exist whether the generations want it or not....

The Church comprises not only the totality of mankind in Christ but as St. Paul and St. John teach, the totality of the world. Thus in the final analysis the Church is the sanctified whole, the new creation in the governance of the Holy Spirit.

On the other hand, the Church does not exist outside the individual but within him. We are—each one of us—members of the Church inasmuch as we belong to it, and individuals inasmuch as we face God alone. It is this Church—this universal Church—which acts and speaks in the Liturgy. It follows that the attitude of the individual when he participates in a liturgical rite and joins in liturgical prayer is different from his attitude in personal prayer.

It is not something beside or in contradiction to the latter but rather is its necessary counterweight in the pattern of Christian existence. Through the Liturgy man steps out of his separateness and becomes part of the whole: a living organ through which the total message of the Church is expressed and enacted.[45]

Cultivating an intentional liturgical life draws us deeply into the Eucharist. Holy Communion is the most intimate act of spousal love. It is the highest, deepest prayer. The spiritual life grows through the complementary grace of liturgical and personal prayer.

WE BECOME WHAT WE RECEIVE

An inner life of contemplation must support the sacramental life. In fact, contemplation is the means through which we "receive," in a strong sense, the mysteries, and through which we interiorize them and open ourselves to their action.

---

[45] Romano Guardini, *The Art of Praying* (Manchester, NH: Sophia Institute Press, 1995), 174–175.

Only when the divine life we receive in the sacraments has been assimilated in contemplation can it be practically expressed in action—in the practice of the virtues and especially in thought. St. Gregory of Nyssa wrote: "There are three facts that manifest a Christian's life and distinguish it: actions, words, thoughts. *Thoughts* come first and then *words* that reveal and manifest what the mind has conceived; last comes *action*, which puts into practice what one has thought."[46]

Contemplation is, then, the set course for passing from communion with Christ in Mass to the imitation of Christ in life.

Prayer

Lord Jesus, through our Eucharistic love and union, in Your gracious kindness, supply what is lacking in me. It is You whom I seek when I imagine happiness. While nothing else satisfies me, You await me with open arms. You are the beauty I desire. You provoke me to thirst for virtue and will not let me settle for compromise. Your Eucharistic love urges me to shed the masks of a false life. When I receive You in the Eucharist, You stir up my desire to do something noble with my life. When I contemplate You in the Eucharistic Mystery, I find new courage to commit myself to patient improvement in the way of love and service. Grant me the grace to become what I receive in the Eucharist. Amen.

---

[46] Raniero Cantalamessa, *The Eucharist, Our Sanctification* (Collegeville, MN: Liturgical Press, 1995), 54.

Prayer Is Essential to Health

Kathleen Beckman

Romano Guardini's teachings on the health benefits of prayer underscore the spiritual benefits of prayer that have been written in this book. Having worked in the medical field for a dozen years, I witnessed the health benefits of Christian prayer. Working with priests in the Church's ministry of healing, deliverance, and exorcism I find it increasingly evident that prayer life brings healing grace for the entire person, soul and body. It is a joy to see the greater collaboration between priests and medical professionals in the care of God's beloved people. I am increasingly aware of the good of such collaboration as a member of the Catholic Medical Association.

There have been many noteworthy pronouncements to the effect that man runs a serious risk if his life is completely devoid of any activity which corresponds or is akin to prayer. Medical authorities point out that people whose attitude is exclusively extrovert, who are carried from one sensation to another, whose thoughts, conversation, work, struggles, and desires are mainly directed toward external goals, soon reach a state of exhaustion and confusion.

To prevent this, life must flow in two directions. It must renew itself from the inner roots, to gather there new strength and resilience. Modern man is in danger of losing his innermost center, which gives stability to his personality and direction to his way of life. Behind the facade of talk and ceaseless activities he becomes unsure of himself; beneath his self-assured *persona* there is an ever-increasing anxiety. To counteract this trend he must rediscover the point of inner support from which he can issue forth into the world and to which he may return again and again.

To regain inner stability it is not sufficient to spend weekends and holidays in the country. A holiday by the sea or in the mountains, no doubt, affords a measure of physical and mental recreation, but it is not true compensation and its effects are soon spent. What is required is a real counterbalance, which is always effective. This cannot be found in purely intellectual pursuits. Poetry, music, and the arts are in themselves not sufficient; nor is philosophy, or any other mental activity. Doctors know this, but to the question of what should be done they usually have no precise answer. Some of them, however, will advocate something in the nature of spiritual or religious practice, some form of contemplative exercise: in short, some form of prayer. This, however, is difficult where faith lacks conviction, for prayer helps only if it is practiced not merely for the sake of its possible effects, but for the sake of the inner relationship with God. It is important that those who believe in this relationship, or who are aware of it, should constantly renew it.

Man needs prayer to remain spiritually healthy. But prayer can spring only from a living faith.[47]

JESUS THE HEALER

The *Catechism of the Catholic Church* sheds light on Jesus as healer and on the Church's charge to continue His ministry, particularly through the sacraments and prayer.

> Often Jesus asks the sick to believe (cf. Mk 5:34, 36, 9:23). He makes use of signs to heal, spittle and the laying on of hands, mud and washing. The sick try to touch him, "for power came forth from him and healed them all" (Lk 6:19, Mk 1:41, 3:10, 6:56). So in the sacraments Christ continues to touch us in order to heal us. (no. 1504)

> Heal the sick! (Mt 10:8). The Church has received this charge from the Lord and strives to carry it out by taking care of the sick as well as by accompanying them with her prayer of intercession. She believes in the life-giving presence of Christ, the physician of souls and bodies. This presence is particularly active through the sacraments, and in an altogether special way through the Eucharist, the bread that gives eternal life and that St. Paul suggests is connected with bodily health (cf. Jn 6:54, 58; 1 Cor 11:30). (no. 1509)

---

[47] Ibid., 6–7.

Prayer to the Divine Physician

Dear Lord Jesus, my Divine Physician, You knit me together in my mother's womb. Thank You for the gift of life; that I am wonderfully made in the image of the Most Holy Trinity. You came to earth to redeem me from sin and death. You came to earth that I may enjoy the abundant life of grace. You came to heal my soul and body. Your healing ministry continues today. O Divine Physician, look with favor upon me, Your servant who is in need of healing, spiritual and physical. Help me to focus on Your healing power, and the gift of medicine and physicians, so I do not succumb to discouragement in my illness. Graciously liberate me from any falsehood regarding my physical being. In faith, hope, and love, I surrender my physical health into Your hands. You are my Creator, and I belong to You. In Your mercy, restore my health in Your way and time. Let Your glory reign in my body and soul. Amen.

About the Authors

Kathleen Beckman is the co-founder of Foundation of Prayer for Priests, an international apostolate of prayer and catechesis, encouraged by the Congregation for Clergy, for holiness of priests and spiritual motherhood (www.foundationforpriests.org). Kathleen is the author of *Praying for Priests: A Mission for the New Evangelization* and *God's Healing Mercy: Finding Your Path to Forgiveness, Peace, and Joy* and a writer for *CatholicExchange*. A frequent guest on Catholic TV and radio, including EWTN and the Catholic Channel, she hosts the Radio Maria program *Eucharist, Mercy, and Saints*. Since 1992, she has served in Magnificat. Since 2000, she has worked with clergy in the Church's ministry of healing, deliverance, and exorcism, serving in the Pope Leo XIII Institute. An Ignatian-certified retreat director, she speaks internationally to clergy, religious, and laity on the spiritual life. A member of the Order of the Holy Sepulchre of Jerusalem, she and her husband are business owners and have two sons and one grandchild. Visit www.kathleenbeckman.com.

Johnnette Benkovic is the founder and president of Women of Grace®, a Catholic apostolate to women that seeks to transform the world, one woman at a time, through spiritual formation. More than forty thousand women internationally have participated in the *Women of Grace* foundational study.

Johnnette hosts the international EWTN weekday television and radio programs *Women of Grace* and *Women of Grace Live*. A sought-after speaker, she presents on various topics in the United States and abroad. Johnnette is also the founder of the Benedicta Leadership Institute for Women®, whose mission is to identify, educate, develop, and train Catholic women to be active leaders and mentors in accord with their state in life. She has developed a certification program and a Masters of Theology program in Catholic Women's Leadership in partnership with SS. Cyril and Methodius Seminary in Orchard Lake, Michigan. Johnnette is the mother of two living children and the grandmother of seven.

Ronda Chervin, Ph.D., is a professor of philosophy at Holy Apostles College and Seminary in Cromwell, Connecticut. She is a prolific writer and an award-winning author of several books. See www.rondachervin.com for more about her writings, some free e-books, and resources.

Pia de Solenni, Ph.D., is a theologian, ethicist, and cultural analyst. She serves as the associate dean of the Augustine Institute, located at Christ Cathedral, Orange, California. She also serves as theological consultant to the Office of the Bishop of Orange County. Dr. de Solenni is an expert in issues relating to women's health, life issues, the new feminism, Catholicism, and culture. Her work has appeared in various publications, including the *Wall Street Journal Europe*, the *Washington Post*, *National Catholic Reporter*, *Our Sunday Visitor*, and *National Review Online*. She is also a consultant member of the Pontifical Academy of St. Thomas Aquinas. Dr. de Solenni received her doctorate in sacred theology summa cum laude from the Pontifical University of the

Holy Cross, Rome. Her dissertation was published in the university series Dissertationes. On November 8, 2001, she received the 2001 Award of the Pontifical Academies for her doctoral work. John Paul II presented the award. She and her husband live in San Diego, California.

Mary Healy, S.T.D., is a professor of Sacred Scripture at Sacred Heart Major Seminary in Detroit and an international speaker on topics related to Scripture, evangelization, healing, and the spiritual life. She is a general editor of the *Catholic Commentary on Sacred Scripture* and the author of two of its volumes, *The Gospel of Mark* and *Hebrews*. Her other books include *Men and Women Are from Eden: A Study Guide to John Paul II's Theology of the Body* and *Healing: Bringing the Gift of God's Mercy to the World*. Dr. Healy is chair of the Doctrinal Commission of International Catholic Charismatic Renewal Services in Rome. She serves the Pontifical Council for Promoting Christian unity as a member of the Pentecostal-Catholic International Dialogue. In 2014 Pope Francis appointed her one of the first three women ever to serve on the Pontifical Biblical Commission.

Lisa M. Hendey is the founder and editor of CatholicMom.com and the bestselling author of *The Grace of Yes*, *The Handbook for Catholic Moms*, and *A Book of Saints for Catholic Moms*. Her partnership with Ave Maria Press, for which she serves as editor-at-large, has resulted in the CatholicMom.com book imprint. Lisa co-edited *The Catholic Mom's Prayer Companion* with eighty co-authors. Her Chime Travelers fiction series for elementary readers, based on the lives of the saints, is being read in Catholic elementary schools and homes nationwide. Lisa has appeared on EWTN, CNN, KNXT, and Catholic TV. She serves as a correspondent and frequent radio guest on numerous outlets. Her articles have appeared in *Catholic Digest, National Catholic Register,* and *Our Sunday Visitor.* Lisa speaks internationally on faith, family, and technology topics. She has traveled worldwide with nonprofit organizations to support their humanitarian missions. She resides in the Archdiocese of Los Angeles.

Joan Lewis, with a B.A. in French from St. Mary's College of Notre Dame, Indiana, and a diploma from the University of Fribourg in Switzerland, taught French for five years in the United States. She moved to Rome and began an extensive journalism career, specializing in the Vatican. She was invited in 1990 to work for the Vatican Information Service in the Holy See Press Office as the English language writer and editor. While working for the Holy See, Joan was named a member of Holy See delegations to United Nations conferences. Appointed Rome Bureau Chief for EWTN in the fall of 2005, she also blogs at *Joan's Rome* (https://joansrome.wordpress.com). Joan is the author of two books, *Jubilee 2000 in Rome* (1999), and *A Holy Year in Rome: The Complete Pilgrim's Guide for the Year of Mercy* (2015). She is a member of the Equestrian Order of the Holy Sepulchre.

Kathryn Jean Lopez is a senior fellow at the National Review Institute, where she directs the Center for Religion, Culture, and Civil Society, and is editor-at-large of *National Review.* She is an award-winding syndicated columnist who speaks frequently on faith and public life and is co-author of *How to Defend the Faith without Raising Your Voice.* She's a contributor to *Angelus, Crux,* and *Our Sunday Visitor Newsweekly,* among other publications.

Marilyn Quirk founded the international women's ministry *Magnificat, A Ministry to Catholic Women,* a private association of the faithful based on the Visitation Scene (www.magnificat-ministry.org). Established in 1981 in the Archdiocese of New Orleans, Magnificat has grown to have more than one hundred international chapters. Marilyn has been featured on EWTN TV and Radio and is a popular conference speaker. She and her husband, Peter, are members of the Knights of the Holy Sepulchre and Legatus. They are proud of their six children and eleven grandchildren. In 2000, Marilyn received the Pontifical award Pro Ecclesia et Pontifice, and in 2016 she received the St. John Paul II Award from the Catholic Leadership Foundation.

Vicki Thorn founded Project Rachel in 1984, and today more than 140 U.S. dioceses offer this post-abortion healing ministry that continues to spread internationally. She travels extensively to speak about Project Rachel. In 2001, Vicki was presented with the Vatican II Award for "Distinguished Service to Society" for her dedication to helping women and men who have been affected by abortion. When she started Project Rachel, Vicki was a young wife and mother with a B.A. in psychology from the University of Minnesota. Her credentials also include being a trauma counselor and a facilitator in bereavement loss and prenatal loss. She and her husband have six children and ten grandchildren.

Kelly Wahlquist is the founder of the national women's ministry WINE: Women in the New Evangelization, the assistant director for the Archbishop Harry J. Flynn Catechetical Institute in the Archdiocese of Saint Paul and Minneapolis, and a contributing writer for Catholicmom.com. Kelly is the author of *Created to Relate: God's Design for Peace and Joy*, which encourages and inspires women to live fully their beautiful God-given gifts for building relationships. She is the editor of *Walk in Her Sandals: Experiencing the Passion of Christ through the Eyes of Women*, a collaborative effort of ten Catholic women writers that looks at six universal gifts of women and guides the reader on a journey through the days of Holy Week, Easter, and Pentecost. Kelly travels the country speaking at Catholic conferences and retreats and leads women's pilgrimages (WINE and Shrine) through Italy. She resides with her husband, Andy, and their three children in Minnesota. Visit KellyWahlquist.com and CatholicVineyard.com.

Sophia Institute

Sophia Institute is a nonprofit institution that seeks to nurture the spiritual, moral, and cultural life of souls and to spread the Gospel of Christ in conformity with the authentic teachings of the Roman Catholic Church.

Sophia Institute Press fulfills this mission by offering translations, reprints, and new publications that afford readers a rich source of the enduring wisdom of mankind.

Sophia Institute also operates two popular online Catholic resources: CrisisMagazine.com and CatholicExchange.com.

Crisis Magazine provides insightful cultural analysis that arms readers with the arguments necessary for navigating the ideological and theological minefields of the day. *Catholic Exchange* provides world news from a Catholic perspective as well as daily devotionals and articles that will help you to grow in holiness and live a life consistent with the teachings of the Church.

In 2013, Sophia Institute launched Sophia Institute for Teachers to renew and rebuild Catholic culture through service to Catholic education. With the goal of nurturing the spiritual, moral, and cultural life of souls, and an abiding respect for the role and work of teachers, we strive to provide materials and programs that are at once enlightening to the mind and ennobling to the heart; faithful and complete, as well as useful and practical.

Sophia Institute gratefully recognizes the Solidarity Association for preserving and encouraging the growth of our apostolate over the course of many years. Without their generous and timely support, this book would not be in your hands.

www.SophiaInstitute.com
www.CatholicExchange.com
www.CrisisMagazine.com
www.SophiaInstituteforTeachers.org

Sophia Institute Press® is a registered trademark of Sophia Institute.
Sophia Institute is a tax-exempt institution as defined by the
Internal Revenue Code, Section 501(c)(3). Tax I.D. 22-2548708.